Writer's Workbook

Level 3

A Division of The McGraw-Hill Companies

Columbus, Ohio

www.sra4kids.com

SRA/McGraw-Hill

A Division of The **McGraw·Hill** *Companies*

Copyright ©2002 by SRA/McGraw-Hill

All rights reserved. Except as permitted under the United States
Copyright Act, no part of this publication may be reproduced or
distributed in any form or by any means, or stored in a database
or retrieval system, without the prior written permission of the
publisher, unless otherwise indicated.

Send all inquiries to:
SRA/McGraw-Hill
8787 Orion Place
Columbus, OH 43240-4027

Printed in the United States of America

ISBN 0-07-569547-2

5 6 7 8 9 QPD 06 05

Table of Contents

Unit 6 Country Life
Personal Writing

Cumulative Checklists

Name _____ Date _____

The Writing Process

Use the writing process to help you make your writing clearer and easier to read.

Prewriting

Who is your audience?

☐ your teacher

☐ your classmates

☐ someone younger than you

☐ your family

☐ other _____

What is your purpose for writing?

☐ to tell a story

☐ to give information

☐ to explain something

☐ to persuade

☐ other _____

What is your task?

☐ to write a description

☐ to write a letter

☐ to write an autobiography

☐ to tell a story

☐ other _____

Objective: Students learn the steps of the writing process and how they can help their writing.

▶ **The Writing Process**

THE WRITING PROCESS

Objective: Students learn the steps of the writing process and how they can help their writing.

Organize your ideas before you begin writing. One way to do this is by using a graphic organizer. One type of graphic organizer is a time line.

Put important dates here.

Put important events for each date here.

Drafting

Write or type the first draft of your writing and put it in your Writing Folder.

▶ **The Writing Process**

Objective: Students learn the steps of the writing process and how they can help their writing.

Revising

Read your writing. Use this checklist to help you revise. Use proofreading marks to make changes.

Ideas

☐ Is the main idea clear?

☐ Do I stay on topic?

☐ Other _____

Organization

☐ Do I follow the order I chose in prewriting?

Word Choice

☐ Do I use some words too many times?

☐ Do I use the best words to describe myself?

Sentence Fluency

☐ Do my sentences read smoothly?

☐ Do I use sentences that are too short or too long?

Voice

☐ Does my writing sound as though I am speaking to my reader?

If the revised draft of your writing has many changes, write your revision on notebook paper and put it in your Writing Folder. If you have typed your draft on a computer, you can use the cut, copy, and paste buttons on the toolbar to move words, sentences, and paragraphs.

Proofreading Marks

¶	Indent.
∧	Add something.
℮	Take out something.
≡	Make a capital letter.
/	Make a small letter.
sp ⟳	Check spelling.
⊙	Add a period.

▶ **The Writing Process**

THE WRITING PROCESS

Objective: Students learn the steps of the writing process and how they can help their writing.

Editing/Proofreading

Always proofread your writing. Mistakes make your writing more difficult to read. Use this checklist to make sure you remember everything.

Conventions

☐ Make sure your words are spelled correctly.

☐ Make sure you have used a capital letter at the beginning of each sentence.

☐ Make sure you have used capital letters for proper nouns.

☐ Make sure every sentence has a punctuation mark at the end.

☐ Check to see that your paragraphs are indented.

☐ Make sure you stay within your margins.

☐ Other _____

Publishing

Use this checklist to make sure your writing is ready to present to your reader.

☐ Make sure your writing says exactly what you want it to say.

☐ Write or type a clean copy of your writing.

☐ Add pictures to your autobiography.

☐ Other _____

UNIT 2 City Wildlife • **Lesson I** *The Boy Who Didn't Believe in Spring*

Objective: Students learn how to write a response to a fiction story.

Responding to Fiction

Use the writing process to write a response to a fiction story.

Prewriting

Who is the audience for your response to fiction?

☐ your teacher

☐ your classmates

☐ your family

☐ other _____

What is your purpose for writing this response to fiction?

☐ to explain your response to the fiction story

☐ to share your thoughts about the fiction story

☐ other _____

Fill in information about the fiction story to which you are responding.

Title: _____

Author: _____

Character, setting, plot, or idea to which you are responding:

_____

Name _____ Date _____

▶ **Responding to Fiction**

Objective: Students learn how to write a response to a fiction story.

EXPOSITORY WRITING

Graphic Organizers

Use this character web to help you organize your thoughts before you write your response to fiction.

☐ Put the character's name in the middle of the web.

☐ In each box, write a thought you have about the character.

☐ Add lines to list details from the story that support each thought.

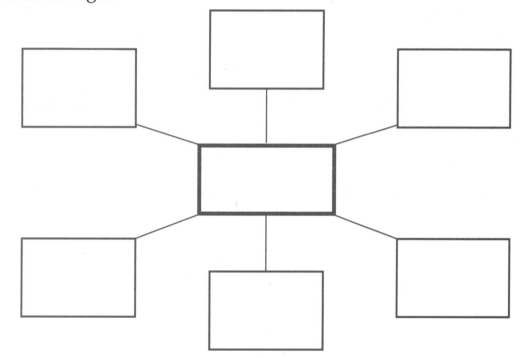

Drafting

Write or type the first draft of your response to fiction and put it in your Writing Folder.

▶ **Responding to Fiction**

Objective: Students learn how to write a response to a fiction story.

Revising

Read your response to fiction. Use the checklist to help you revise. Use proofreading marks to make changes.

Proofreading Marks

Mark	Meaning
¶	Indent.
∧	Add something.
ℓ	Take out something.
≡	Make a capital letter.
/	Make a small letter.
sp ⟲	Check spelling.
⊙	Add a period.

Ideas

☐ Do you have a topic sentence for each paragraph?

Organization

☐ Do all of the sentences in each paragraph support the topic of the paragraph?

Word Choice

☐ Did you use time and order words to make your writing clearer?

Sentence Fluency

☐ Do you have both long and short sentences?

Voice

☐ Read your response to fiction. Does your writing sound as though you liked, or disliked, the fiction story you read?

☐ Other _____

If your revised draft has many changes, write out your revision and put it in your Writing Folder. If you have typed your draft on a computer, you can use the cut, copy, and paste buttons on the toolbar to move words, sentences, and paragraphs.

▶ **Responding to Fiction**

Objective: Students learn how to write a response to a fiction story.

EXPOSITORY WRITING

Editing/Proofreading

Edit/Proofread your response on notebook paper or on a computer, and put it in your Writing Folder. Read your response carefully. Use the checklist to help you correct any mistakes. Make your writing smooth and easy to read.

Conventions

☐ Are the names of the story's characters and places spelled correctly?

☐ Do direct quotes have commas and quotation marks in the proper places? Is each quote indented?

☐ Are the paragraphs indented?

☐ Is the story title underlined and capitalized?

☐ Other _____

Publishing

Use the checklist to get your response ready to share.

Presentation

☐ Write or type a neat final copy of your response.

☐ Add a drawing, map, or computer graphics.

☐ Other _____

Summary Paragraph

Objective: Students learn how to write summaries.

Use the writing process to write a summary paragraph.

Prewriting

Who is the audience for your summary paragraph?

☐ your teacher

☐ your classmates

☐ other _____

What is your purpose for writing this summary paragraph?

☐ to share or explain what you have learned about something you read

☐ to show your understanding of what you read

☐ other _____

Fill in the information for the article or book you are summarizing.

Title: _____

Author: _____

Subject of article or book: _____

_____

Objective: Students learn how to write summaries.

Graphic Organizers

▶ **Summary Paragraph**

Use this expository structure to help you organize your ideas before you begin writing the first draft of your summary.

☐ Write the main idea of the article or book you are summarizing in the *Topic* box.

☐ Put other important ideas, such as examples, reasons, and facts, in the *Subtopic* boxes.

☐ Write the conclusion of the article in the *Conclusion* box.

Expository Structure

```
              ┌──────────┐
              │  Topic   │
      ┌───────┴──────────┴───────┐
      │                          │
      └──────────────────────────┘

   ┌──────────┐          ┌──────────┐
   │ Subtopic │          │ Subtopic │
 ┌─┴──────────┴─┐      ┌─┴──────────┴─┐
 │              │      │              │
 └──────────────┘      └──────────────┘

          ┌────────────┐
          │ Conclusion │
      ┌───┴────────────┴───┐
      │                    │
      │                    │
      └────────────────────┘
```

Drafting

Write or type the first draft of your paragraph and put it in your Writing Folder.

EXPOSITORY WRITING

Objective: Students learn how to write summaries.

▶ **Summary Paragraph**

Revising

Read the first draft of your summary paragraph. Use the checklist to help you revise. Use proofreading marks to make changes and corrections.

Proofreading Marks

¶	Indent.
∧	Add something.
℮	Take out something.
≡	Make a capital letter.
/	Make a small letter.
ⓈⓅ	Check spelling.
⊙	Add a period.

Ideas

☐ Is the main idea stated in the first sentence?

Organization

☐ Take out any information you did not get from the article or book.

Word Choice

☐ Did you use time and order words to help readers follow the order of events?

Sentence Fluency

☐ Did you begin your sentences in different ways?

Voice

☐ Does your writing sound serious and informative?

☐ Other _____

If your revised draft has many changes, write out your revision and put it in your Writing Folder. If you have typed your draft on a computer, you can use the cut, copy, and paste buttons on the toolbar to move words, sentences, and paragraphs.

▶ **Summary Paragraph**

Objective: Students learn how to write summaries.

EXPOSITORY WRITING

Editing/Proofreading

Edit/proofread your summary paragraph on notebook paper or on a computer and put it in your Writing Folder. Read your paragraph carefully. Use the checklist to help you correct any mistakes. Make your writing easy to read and understand.

Conventions

☐ Are all words spelled correctly?

☐ Are the paragraphs indented?

☐ Be sure to capitalize the title of the book or article you are summarizing.

☐ Are book titles underlined and article titles put in quotation marks?

☐ Have you used commas correctly between words or phrases in a series?

☐ Other _____

Publishing

Use the checklist to get your paragraph ready to share.

Presentation

☐ Write or type a neat final copy of your summary.

☐ Other _____

Book Review

Use the writing process to write a book review of a fiction or nonfiction book you have read.

Prewriting

Who is the audience for your book review?

☐ your teacher

☐ your classmates

☐ your family

☐ people who read book reviews in magazines

☐ other _____

What is your purpose for writing this review?

☐ to explain about the book that you read

☐ to recommend, or not recommend, the book to other people

☐ other _____

Fill in information about the book.

Title of book: _____

Author: _____

Subject of book: _____

_____

Objective: Students learn the tools needed to write a book review.

▶ **Book Review**

EXPOSITORY WRITING

Objective: Students learn the tools needed to write a book review.

Graphic Organizers

Use this story map to organize your ideas for a book review.

☐ Use the space below to give your opinion or recommendation.

☐ List reasons or details that support your opinion.

Story Map

Title:

Characters:

Setting:

Plot (What Happened)

Beginning (Problem): _____

Middle (Events): 1. _____

2. _____

Ending (How the problem was solved): _____

Opinion _____

Reasons & Details _____

Drafting

Write or type the first draft of your review and put it in your Writing Folder.

Objective: Students learn the tools needed to write a book review.

▶ **Book Review**

Revising

Read the first draft of your book review. Use the checklist to help you revise. Use proofreading marks to make changes and corrections.

Proofreading Marks

¶	Indent.
∧	Add something.
ℓ	Take out something.
≡	Make a capital letter.
/	Make a small letter.
⬭ sp	Check spelling.
⊙	Add a period.

Ideas

☐ Do you use reasons and details to support your opinion and recommendation?

☐ Do you state the problem or main idea of the plot in the first sentence of the first paragraph?

Organization

☐ Did you follow the order of events in the story?

Word Choice

☐ Do you use time and order words to help your readers follow the action?

Sentence Fluency

☐ Are your sentences smooth and easy to read?

Voice

☐ Does your review sound as though you liked or disliked the book?

☐ Other_____

If your revised draft has many changes, write your revisions on paper and put it in your Writing Folder. If you typed the draft on a computer, you can use the cut, copy, and paste buttons on the toolbar to move words, sentences, and paragraphs.

▶ **Book Review**

Objective: Students learn the tools needed to write a book review.

Editing/Proofreading

Edit/proofread your book review on notebook paper or a computer and put it in your Writing Folder. Read your book review carefully. Use the checklist to help you correct any mistakes. Make your writing easy to read and understand.

Conventions

☐ Are the title of the book and the author's name spelled correctly?

☐ Is the book title underlined and capitalized correctly?

☐ Are all your paragraphs indented?

☐ Do you use the correct punctuation for quotations?

☐ Other_____

Publishing

Use the checklist to get your book review ready to share.

Presentation

☐ Write or type a neat and clean final copy of your book review.

☐ Add a drawing, map, computer graphic, or photo.

☐ Send your book review to a children's magazine.

☐ Other _____

EXPOSITORY WRITING

UNIT 2   City Wildlife • **Lesson 4** *Urban Roosts*

Responding to Nonfiction

Use the writing process to write a response to a nonfiction article or book.

Prewriting

Who is the audience?

☐ your teacher

☐ your classmates

☐ other _____

What is your purpose for writing?

☐ to explain your response to the nonfiction work
you read

☐ to show your understanding of the nonfiction
work you read

☐ other _____

**Fill in the information about the nonfiction
article or book you have chosen.**

Title: _____

Author: _____

Subject of nonfiction article or book: _____

_____

UNIT 2 City Wildlife • **Lesson 4** *Urban Roosts*

Objective: Students learn how to share their responses to nonfiction.

▶ **Responding to Nonfiction**

Graphic Organizers

Use this expository structure graphic organizer to organize your thoughts.

☐ Under *Topic*, write the main idea of the work.

☐ Under *Subtopic*, list the examples, reasons, or facts that support the main idea or topic.

Expository Structure

> **Topic**
> [ ]

> **Subtopic**
> [ ]

> **Subtopic**
> [ ]

1._____

1._____

_____

_____

2._____

2._____

_____

_____

> **My Opinion**
> [ ]

Drafting

Write or type the first draft of your response to nonfiction and put it in your Writing Folder.

EXPOSITORY WRITING

Name _____ Date _____

▶ **Responding to Nonfiction**

Revising

Read the first draft of your response to nonfiction. Use the checklist to help you revise. Use proofreading marks to make changes and corrections.

Ideas

☐ Do you use reasons and details to support your thoughts?

Organization

☐ Do all the sentences in a paragraph support the topic of the paragraph?

Word Choice

☐ Are your words clear and specific?

Sentence Fluency

☐ Do you begin your sentences in different ways?

☐ Do you have some long and some short sentences?

Voice

☐ Does your writing sound as though you liked or disliked the article or book?

☐ Other _____

If your revised draft has many changes, write it on paper or type it on a computer and put it in your Writing Folder.

Proofreading Marks	
¶	Indent.
∧	Add something.
℮	Take out something.
≡	Make a capital letter.
/	Make a small letter.
sp⟲	Check spelling.
⊙	Add a period.

Objective: Students learn how to share their responses to nonfiction.

▶ **Responding to Nonfiction**

Editing/Proofreading

Edit/proofread your response to nonfiction on notebook paper or on a computer and put it in your Writing Folder. Read your response to nonfiction carefully. Use the checklist to help you correct any mistakes. Make your writing easy to read and understand.

Conventions

☐ Are the main words of the title of the article or book capitalized?

☐ Are the title of the article or book and the author's name spelled correctly?

☐ Is the book title underlined, or the article title in quotation marks?

☐ Other _____

Publishing

Use the checklist to get your response ready to share.

Presentation

☐ Write or type a neat and clean final copy of your response to nonfiction.

☐ Add a drawing, map, or computer graphic to add interest to your response.

☐ Other _____

Objective: Students learn how to share their responses to nonfiction.

EXPOSITORY WRITING

Explain a Process

Objective: Students learn the tools needed to explain a process.

Use the writing process to explain a process.

Prewriting

Who is the audience for your explanation of a process?

☐ your teacher

☐ your friends or classmates

☐ your family

☐ a younger child

☐ other _____

What is your purpose for writing this explanation of a process?

☐ to tell someone how to do something

☐ to share how you did something

☐ other _____

What process are you going to explain?

_____

Name _____ Date _____

▶ **Explain a Process**

Graphic Organizers

Use the chain of events graphic organizer to help you organize the steps of the process you are explaining.

☐ Put the first step in the first box, and then follow the arrows to write the next steps in order.

☐ You can number the steps to help keep track of the exact order.

Chain of Events in _____

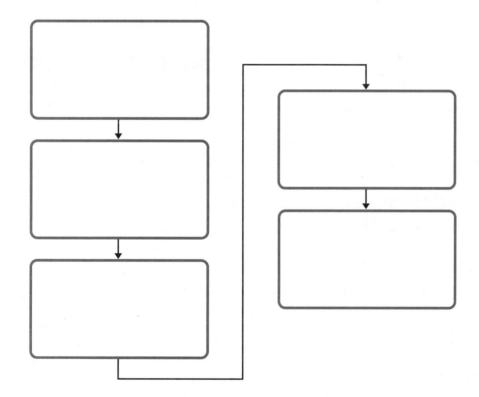

Drafting

Write or type the first draft of your explanation of a process and put it in your Writing Folder.

Objective: Students learn the tools needed to explain a process.

EXPOSITORY WRITING

UNIT 2 City Wildlife • **Lesson 5** *Two Days in May*

► **Explain a Process**

Revising

Read the first draft of your explanation of a process. Use the checklist to help you revise. Use editing and proofreading marks to make changes and corrections.

Ideas

☐ Did you include all the necessary steps?

Organization

☐ Are the sentences in the best order to help readers understand the process?

Word Choice

☐ Are your words clear and specific so readers will understand the steps?

☐ Did you choose words that your audience will understand?

Sentence Fluency

☐ Did you make your sentences different lengths so your writing sounds smooth?

Voice

☐ Is your writing informative and easy to understand?

☐ Other _____

If your revised draft has many changes, write it on paper and put it in your Writing Folder. If you have typed your draft on a computer, you can use the cut, copy, and paste buttons on the toolbar to move words, sentences, and paragraphs.

Proofreading Marks

¶	Indent.
∧	Add something.
	Take out something.
≡	Make a capital letter.
/	Make a small letter.
sp	Check spelling.
⊙	Add a period.

Objective: Students learn the tools needed to explain a process.

▶ **Explain a Process**

EXPOSITORY WRITING

Objective: Students learn the tools needed to explain a process.

Editing/Proofreading

Edit/proofread your explanation on notebook paper or on a computer and put it in your Writing Folder. Read your explanation carefully. Use the checklist to help you correct any mistakes. Make your writing easy to read and understand.

Conventions

☐ Are all your words spelled correctly?

☐ Did you use question marks and exclamation points where needed?

☐ Did you capitalize the title?

☐ Are all the paragraphs indented?

☐ Other _____

Publishing

Use the checklist to get your explanation ready to share.

Presentation

☐ Write or type a neat final copy of your explanation.

☐ Add a drawing or computer graphics to aid in your explanation.

☐ Other _____

UNIT 2 City Wildlife • **Lesson 6** *Secret Place*

Research Report

Objective: Students learn the process of writing a research report.

Use the writing process to write a research report.

Prewriting

Who is the audience for your research report?

☐ your teacher

☐ your classmates

☐ your family

☐ other _____

What is your purpose for writing this research report?

☐ to show what you have learned about a subject

☐ to inform others about a subject

☐ other _____

What is your topic for your research report?

_____

What are your sources of information?

☐ nonfiction books

☐ encyclopedias (books or electronic)

☐ magazines or newspapers

☐ dictionary

☐ atlas

☐ other _____

EXPOSITORY WRITING

► **Research Report**

Objective: Students learn the process of writing a research report.

Graphic Organizers

Use this expository structure graphic organizer to help you remember and organize the information you have gathered for your report.

☐ Write a phrase about your topic in the *Topic* box.

☐ Under *Subtopic*, write a word or short phrase telling the topic of that paragraph.

☐ In the *Conclusion* box, summarize the topic of your report.

Expository Structure

```
                    ┌─────────────┐
                    │    Topic     │
        ┌───────────┴─────────────┴───────────┐
        │                                       │
        └───────────────────────────────────────┘

        ┌──────────────┐        ┌──────────────┐
        │   Subtopic    │        │   Subtopic    │
   ┌────┴──────────────┴───┐  ┌──┴──────────────┴───┐
   │                        │  │                      │
   │                        │  │                      │
   │                        │  │                      │
   └────────────────────────┘  └──────────────────────┘

                    ┌─────────────┐
                    │  Conclusion  │
        ┌───────────┴─────────────┴───────────┐
        │                                       │
        │                                       │
        └───────────────────────────────────────┘
```

Drafting

Write or type the first draft of your research report and put it in your Writing Folder.

UNIT 2 City Wildlife • **Lesson 6** *Secret Place*

Objective: Students learn the process of writing a research report.

▶ Research Report

Revising

Read the first draft of your research report. Use the checklist to help you revise. Use editing and proofreading marks to make changes and corrections.

Ideas

☐ Do you have an effective beginning?

☐ Did you sum up your report in a conclusion?

Organization

☐ Are sentences and paragraphs in the best order for reading and understanding?

Word Choice

☐ Did you explain or define any uncommon words or terms?

Sentence Fluency

☐ Did you begin your sentences in different ways to make them more interesting?

Voice

☐ Is your writing informative and easy to understand?

☐ Other _____

Proofreading Marks

¶	Indent.
∧	Add something.
ℓ	Take out something.
≡	Make a capital letter.
/	Make a small letter.
sp	Check spelling.
⊙	Add a period.

If your revised draft has many changes, write it on paper and put it in your Writing Folder. If you have typed your draft on a computer, you can use the cut, copy, and paste buttons on the toolbar to move words, sentences, and paragraphs.

▸ **Research Report**

EXPOSITORY WRITING

Objective: Students learn the process of writing a research report.

Editing/Proofreading

Edit/proofread your research report on notebook paper or on a computer and put it in your Writing Folder. Read your report carefully. Use the checklist to help you correct any mistakes. Make your writing easy to read and understand.

Conventions

- ☐ Are all words spelled correctly?
- ☐ Are all the paragraphs indented?
- ☐ Are the names of people and places capitalized?

- ☐ Other _____

Publishing

Use the checklist to make your writing look its best.

Presentation

- ☐ Write or type a neat final copy of your research report.
- ☐ Add a drawing, map, computer graphic, chart, or photo to add interest to your research report.

- ☐ Other _____

Sensory Description

Use the writing process to write a sensory description.

Prewriting

Who is the audience for your sensory description?

☐ your teacher

☐ your classmates

☐ your parent

☐ other _____

What is your purpose for writing this sensory description?

☐ to describe something using senses other than sight

☐ to share a sensory description with others

☐ other _____

What thing are you going to describe?

_____

UNIT 3 Imagination • **Lesson I** *Through Grandpa's Eyes*

▶ **Sensory Description**

Objective: Students prewrite and draft a sensory description.

DESCRIPTIVE POETRY

A character web graphic organizer is good to use for a sensory description. You can adapt the character web if you are using a variety of senses in your description.

• Write the name of the thing or subject you are describing in the middle box.

• Write sensory details in the little boxes. Remember to use sensory adjectives.

Character Web

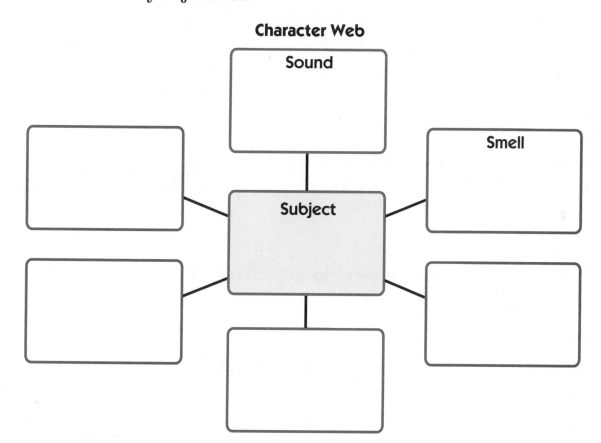

Sound

Smell

Subject

Drafting

Write the first draft of your sensory description on paper or type it on a computer, and put it in your **Writing Folder.**

Objective: Students revise a sensory description.

Revising

▶ **Sensory Description**

Read the first draft of your sensory description. Use the checklist to help you revise your writing. Use editing and proofreading marks to make changes and corrections.

Ideas

☐ Does your description give a clear and complete picture of your subject?

☐ Did you use several different senses to describe your subject?

Organization

☐ Did you organize the details in a way that makes your description easy to understand?

Word Choice

☐ Did you use a variety of sensory adjectives to keep your reader's interest?

Sentence Fluency

☐ Did you make your sentences different lengths so they are more interesting to read?

Voice

☐ Read your description out loud. Does it sound like you know the subject of your sensory description well?

If your revised draft has many changes, write or type your revision on paper and put it in your Writing Folder.

Proofreading Marks

¶	Indent.
∧	Add something.
	Take out something.
≡	Make a capital letter.
/	Make a small letter.
	Check spelling.
⊙	Add a period.
∧	Add a comma.

Sensory Description

DESCRIPTIVE POETRY

Objective: Students edit/proofread and publish a sensory description.

Editing/Proofreading

Edit your sensory description on paper or computer. Then make a clean copy of your description, and put it in your Writing Folder. Read your sensory description carefully. Use the checklist to help you correct any mistakes.

Conventions

☐ Are all your adjectives spelled correctly? Use a dictionary if you are unsure of spelling.

☐ Did you use commas when listing two or more adjectives?

☐ Did you capitalize the title of your sensory description?

☐ Are the paragraphs indented?

Publishing

Use the checklist to make your writing look its best.

Presentation

☐ Write or type a neat final copy of your description.

☐ Include a drawing, map, or computer graphics to add interest to your writing.

☐ Practice reading your sensory description out loud if you plan to give an oral presentation.

Rhyming Poem—Couplet or Triplet

Use the writing process to write a couplet or triplet rhyming poem.

Prewriting

Who is the audience for your rhyming poem?

☐ your teacher

☐ your classmates

☐ your parent

☐ a younger child

☐ other _____

What is your purpose for writing this couplet or triplet rhyming poem?

☐ to explain your thoughts or feelings in a poem

☐ to entertain others with a poem

☐ other _____

What is the subject, thought, or feeling you are writing a poem about?

_____

Objective: Students learn how to write a couplet or triplet poem.

UNIT 3 Imagination • **Lesson 2** *The Cat Who Became a Poet*

▶ Rhyming Poem—Couplet or Triplet

DESCRIPTIVE POETRY

Objective: Students prewrite and draft a couplet or triplet poem.

A top-to-bottom graphic organizer is a good one to use for a couplet or triplet rhyming poem.

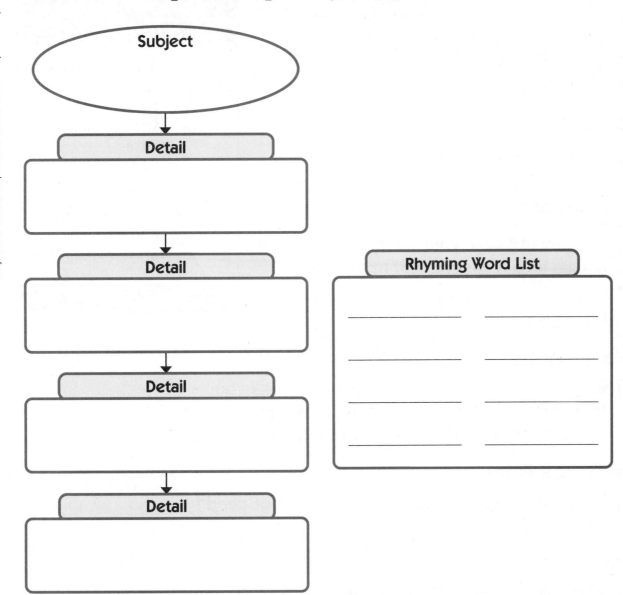

Subject

Detail

Detail

Detail

Detail

Rhyming Word List

Drafting

Write or type the first draft of your couplet or triplet rhyming poem on paper or type it on a computer, and put it in your Writing Folder.

Objective: Students revise a couplet or triplet poem.

Revising

▶ Rhyming Poem—Couplet or Triplet

Read the first draft of your couplet or triplet rhyming poem. Use the checklist to help you revise your poem. Use proofreading marks to make changes and corrections.

Ideas

☐ Does your poem serve your purpose, to explain or entertain?

Organization

☐ Did you organize your poem in a way that makes it easy to read and understand?

☐ Did you put rhyming words at the end of the lines?

Word Choice

☐ Did you choose the best words to express your thoughts and feelings? You can use a dictionary or thesaurus to give you more word choices.

Sentence Fluency

☐ Do your lines sound smooth? They do not need to be complete sentences.

Voice

☐ Does your poem get your feelings across to your readers?

If your revised draft has many changes, write or type it and put it in your Writing Folder.

Proofreading Marks	
∧	Add something.
ℓ	Take out something.
≡	Make a capital letter.
/	Make a small letter.
ˢᵖ	Check spelling.
⊙	Add a period.
∧	Add a comma.

Objective: Students edit/proofread and publish a couplet or triplet poem.

DESCRIPTIVE POETRY

▶ **Rhyming Poem—Couplet or Triplet**

Editing/Proofreading

Edit your rhyming poem on paper or computer. Then make a clean copy of your poem, and put it in your Writing Folder. Read your rhyming poem carefully. Use the checklist to help you correct any mistakes.

Conventions

☐ Are all of your words spelled correctly? Use a dictionary if you are unsure of spelling.

☐ Did you use commas and periods to make pauses in your poem? Punctuation is not necessary in poetry, but you can use it for added effect.

☐ Did you add apostrophes in the proper place in contractions?

☐ Did you capitalize the title?

Publishing

Use the checklist to make your writing look its best.

Presentation

☐ Write or type a neat final copy of your rhyming poem.

☐ Include a drawing, a photograph, or computer graphics to add interest to your poem.

☐ Practice reading your rhyming poem out loud if you plan to give an oral presentation.

Top-to-Bottom Description

Objective: Students learn to write a top-to-bottom description.

Use the writing process to write a top-to-bottom description.

Prewriting

Who is the audience for your top-to-bottom description?

☐ your teacher

☐ your classmates

☐ your parent

☐ other _____

What is your purpose for writing this top-to-bottom description?

☐ to organize a description to make it easy to understand and remember

☐ to give the reader a clear picture of something

☐ other _____

What is the subject of your description?

_____

Name _____ Date _____

Objective: Students prewrite and draft a top-to-bottom description.

Top-to-Bottom Description

Use the top-to-bottom graphic organizer below
to help you organize your top-to-bottom
description.

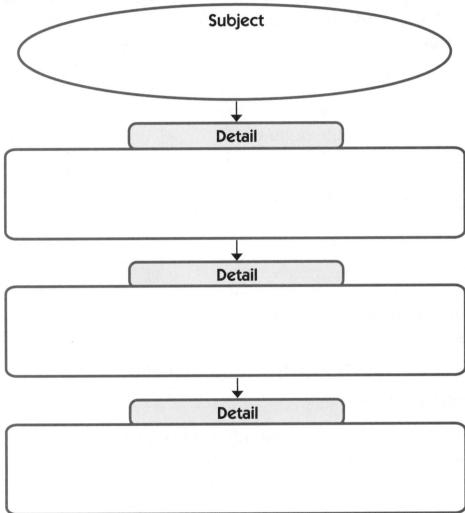

Subject

Detail

Detail

Detail

Drafting

Write or type the first draft of your top-to-bottom
description and put it in your Writing Folder.

DESCRIPTIVE POETRY

UNIT 3 Imagination • **Lesson 3** *A Cloak for the Dreamer*

▶ **Top-to-Bottom Description**

Revising

Read the first draft of your top-to-bottom description. Use the checklist to help you revise your description. Use editing and proofreading marks to make changes and corrections.

Ideas

☐ Does your description include all the details from your graphic organizer?

Organization

☐ Did you organize your descriptive details top-to-bottom?

Word Choice

☐ Do your place and location words make it clear to readers where people, things, and actions are?

☐ Have you used the correct tense of all your verbs?

Sentence Fluency

☐ Did you begin your sentences in different ways to make your description more interesting to read?

Voice

☐ Read your description. Does your top-to-bottom description sound like you know your subject well?

If your revised draft has many changes, write or type it out and put it in your Writing Folder.

Proofreading Marks

 Indent.
 Add something.
 Take out something.
 Make a capital letter.
 Make a small letter.
 Check spelling.
 Add a period.
∧ Add a comma.

Top-to-Bottom Description

Objective: Students edit/proofread and publish a top-to-bottom description.

Editing/Proofreading

Read your top-to-bottom description carefully. Use the checklist to help you correct any mistakes. Make your writing easy to read and understand.

Conventions

☐ Are all your verb tenses spelled correctly? Use a dictionary if you are unsure of spelling.

☐ Did you use commas and end punctuation correctly?

☐ Have you capitalized the title of your description and any proper names and places?

☐ Are the paragraphs indented?

Publishing

Use the checklist to make your writing look its best.

Presentation

☐ Write or type a neat final copy of your top-to-bottom description.

☐ Include a drawing, a map, or computer graphics to add interest to your writing.

☐ Practice reading your top-to-bottom description out loud if you plan to give an oral presentation.

Objective: Students learn how to write a free-verse poem.

Nonrhyming Poetry—Free Verse

Use the writing process to write a free-verse poem.

Prewriting

Who is the audience for your free-verse poem?

☐ your teacher

☐ your classmates

☐ your parent

☐ other _____

What is your purpose for writing this free-verse poem?

☐ to explain your thoughts or feelings in a poem

☐ to entertain others with a poem

☐ other _____

What is the subject, thought, or feeling you are writing about in this poem?

_____

_____

Nonrhyming Poetry—Free Verse

Use this web graphic organizer to help you
organize and remember the thoughts and
feelings for your free-verse poem.
- Write the subject of your poem in the middle box.
- Write thoughts, feelings, or details in the boxes
  around the middle box.

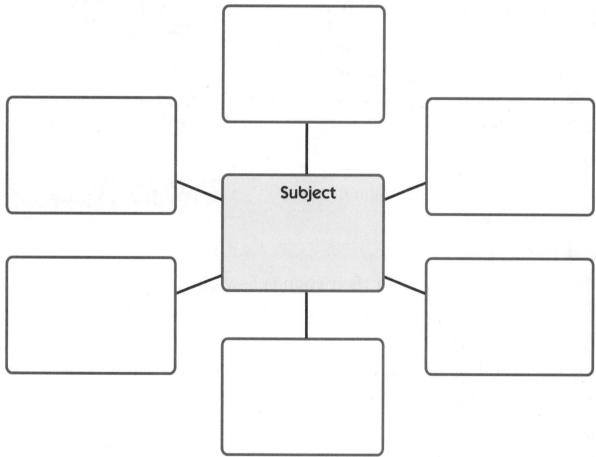

Subject

Objective: Students learn to prewrite and draft a free-verse poem.

DESCRIPTIVE POETRY

Drafting

Write the first draft of your free-verse poem and
put it in your Writing Folder.

Revising

▶ **Nonrhyming Poetry—Free Verse**

Read the first draft of your free-verse poem. Use the checklist to help you revise your writing. Use editing and proofreading marks to make changes and corrections.

Ideas

☐ Does your poem include the ideas, feelings, or thoughts you want?

☐ Does your poem serve your purpose, to explain or entertain?

Organization

☐ Did you organize your poem in a way that is easy to read?

Word Choice

☐ Did you choose words for their sounds as well as their meanings?

Sentence Fluency

☐ Do the lines of your poem sound smooth? They do not need to be complete sentences.

Voice

☐ Read your free-verse poem out loud. Does it sound like you are entertaining or explaining?

If your revised draft has many changes, write or type your revision and put it in your Writing Folder.

Proofreading Marks	
∧	Add something.
ℓ	Take out something.
≡	Make a capital letter.
/	Make a small letter.
sp	Check spelling.
⊙	Add a period.
∧	Add a comma.

Objective: Students learn how to revise a free verse poem.

UNIT 3 Imagination • **Lesson 4** *Picasso*

Nonrhyming Poetry—Free Verse

Objective: Students learn how to edit/proofread and publish a free verse poem.

DESCRIPTIVE POETRY

Editing/Proofreading

**Edit your free-verse poem on paper or computer.
Then make a clean copy of your poem, and put it
in your Writing Folder. Read your free-verse
poem out loud carefully. Use the checklist to help
you correct any mistakes.**

Conventions

☐ Are all your words spelled correctly? Use a
dictionary if you are unsure of the spelling.

☐ Did you use commas and end punctuation to make
pauses in your poem? Punctuation is not required
in free-verse poetry, but you can use it for added
effect.

☐ Did you capitalize the title?

Publishing

**Use the checklist to get your poem ready to
share.**

Presentation

☐ Write or type a neat final copy of your free-verse
poem.

☐ Include a drawing, photograph, or computer
graphics to your poem.

☐ Practice reading your free-verse poem out loud if
you plan to give an oral presentation.

Name _____ Date _____

Objective: Students learn how to compose a quatrain poem.

Rhyming Poem— Quatrain

Use the writing process to write a quatrain rhyming poem.

Prewriting

Who is the audience for your quatrain poem?

☐ your teacher

☐ your classmates

☐ your parent

☐ other _____

What is your purpose for writing this rhyming poem?

☐ to explain your thoughts or feelings in a poem

☐ to entertain others with a poem

☐ other _____

What is the subject, thought, or feeling you are writing about in this quatrain poem?

_____

_____

UNIT 3 Imagination • **Lesson 5** *The Emperor's New Clothes*

DESCRIPTIVE POETRY

Objective: Students learn how to prewrite and draft a quatrain poem.

▶ **Rhyming Poem—Quatrain**

Use this top-to-bottom graphic organizer to help
you organize the lines of your poem, and help
you remember the details, thoughts, and feelings
you want to include.

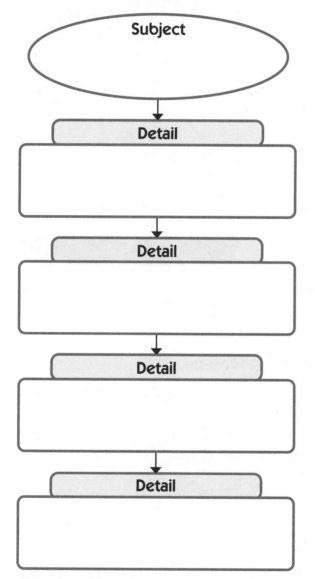

Subject

Detail

Detail

Detail

Detail

Rhyming Word List

_____ _____

_____ _____

_____ _____

_____ _____

Drafting

Write the first draft of your quatrain poem on
paper or on a computer, and put it in your
Writing Folder.

UNIT 3 Imagination • **Lesson 5** *The Emperor's New Clothes*

Revising

▶ **Rhyming Poem—Quatrain**

Read the first draft of your quatrain poem. Use the checklist to help you revise your poem. Use editing and proofreading marks to make changes and corrections.

Ideas

☐ Does your poem include all the details, thoughts, and feelings you want?

Organization

☐ Did you follow a rhyming pattern?

Word Choice

☐ Did you choose the best words to express your thoughts and feelings? Sensory adjectives and figurative language help make your writing more interesting to read.

☐ Did you choose words for their sounds as well as their meanings?

Sentence Fluency

☐ Do your lines sound smooth? They do not need to be complete sentences.

Voice

☐ Do your feelings come through in the poem?

If your revised draft of your poem has many changes, write or type your revision and put it in your Writing Folder.

Proofreading Marks	
∧	Add something.
ℓ	Take out something.
≡	Make a capital letter.
/	Make a small letter.
⟋	Check spelling.
⊙	Add a period.
∧	Add a comma.

Objective: Students learn how to revise a quatrain poem.

▶ **Rhyming Poem—Quatrain**

DESCRIPTIVE POETRY

Objective: Students learn how to edit/proofread and publish a quatrain poem.

Editing/Proofreading

Edit your quatrain poem on paper or on computer. Then make a clean copy of your poem, and put it in your Writing Folder. Read your quatrain poem carefully. Use the checklist to help you correct any mistakes.

Conventions

☐ Did you use the correct article for each noun?

☐ Are all your words spelled correctly? Use a dictionary if you are unsure of the spelling.

☐ Did you use commas and end punctuation to make pauses in your poem? Punctuation is not required in poetry, but you can use it for added effect.

☐ Did you capitalize the title?

Publishing

Use the checklist to get your poem ready to share.

Presentation

☐ Write or type a neat final copy of your quatrain poem.

☐ Include a drawing, a photograph, or computer graphics to add interest to your poem.

☐ Practice reading your quatrain poem out loud if you plan to give an oral presentation.

Sensory Description of a Place

Objective: Students learn how to describe a place.

Use the writing process to write a sensory description of a place.

Prewriting

Who is the audience for your sensory description of a place?

☐ your teacher

☐ your classmates

☐ your parent

☐ a younger child

☐ other _____

What is your purpose for writing this description?

☐ to give readers a clear picture of a special place

☐ to share why a place is special to you

☐ other _____

Name the place you want to write about in this description.

_____

UNIT 3 Imagination • **Lesson 6** *Roxaboxen*

▶ **Sensory Description of a Place**

Use this web graphic organizer to help you organize the details of your sensory description of a place.

- Write the subject of your description in the middle box.
- Write sensory details in the little boxes. Remember to use a variety of sensory adjectives.

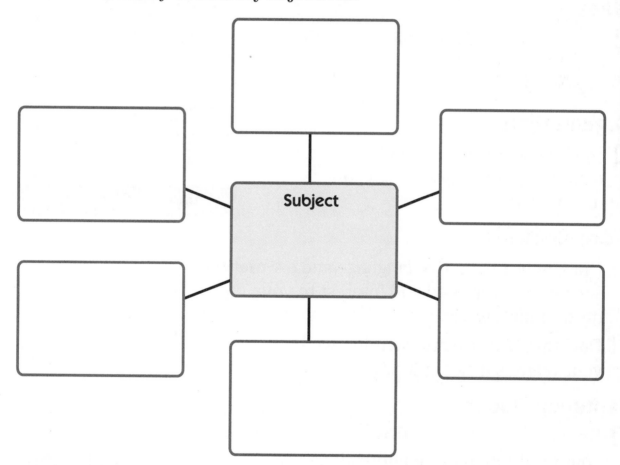

Subject

Drafting

Write or type the first draft of your description and put it in your Writing Folder.

Objective: Students learn how to prewrite and draft a description of a place.

DESCRIPTIVE POETRY

Objective: Students learn how to revise a description of a place.

▶ Sensory Description of a Place

Revising

Read the first draft of your sensory description of a place. Use the checklist to help you revise your description. Use editing and proofreading marks to make changes and corrections.

Ideas

☐ Does your description include all the details you want from your graphic organizer?

Organization

☐ Did you organize the details in a way that makes your description easy to understand?

Word Choice

☐ Did you use figurative language and a variety of sensory adjectives to add interest to your description?

☐ Did you use place and location words to help give your readers a clear picture?

Sentence Fluency

☐ Do your sentences begin in different ways to make your description more interesting to read?

Voice

☐ Does your description sound like you know the place well?

If your revised draft has many changes, write or type your revision and put it in your Writing Folder.

Proofreading Marks	
¶	Indent.
∧	Add something.
ℯ	Take out something.
≡	Make a capital letter.
/	Make a small letter.
℘	Check spelling.
⊙	Add a period.
∧	Add a comma.

Objective: Students edit/proofread and publish a description of a place.

DESCRIPTIVE POETRY

▶ Sensory Description of a Place

Editing/Proofreading

Edit your sensory description of a place on paper or computer. Then make a clean copy of your description, and put it in your Writing Folder. Read your sensory description of a place carefully. Use the checklist to help you correct any mistakes.

Conventions

☐ Did you capitalize the proper names of people and places?

☐ Are all the proper names of people and places spelled correctly?

☐ Did you use the correct verb tenses and articles for nouns?

☐ When you combined sentences, did you use the correct conjunction? Did you use a comma before the conjunction?

Publishing

Use the checklist to make your writing look its best.

Presentation

☐ Write or type a neat final copy of your sensory description of a place.

☐ Include a drawing, map, or computer graphics to add interest to your description.

☐ Practice reading your sensory description out loud if you plan to give an oral presentation.

UNIT 4 Money • **Lesson I** *A New Coat for Anna*

Writing a Persuasive Letter

Use the writing process to write a persuasive letter.

Prewriting

Who is the audience for your persuasive letter?

☐ your teacher

☐ your brother or sister

☐ your parent

☐ other _____

What is your purpose for writing a persuasive letter?

☐ to persuade someone to trade something with me

☐ to persuade someone to vote for me

☐ to persuade someone to help with a special project

☐ other _____

Write the name and address of the person to whom you will send your letter:

Name: _____

Address: _____

_____

Objective: Students learn how to write a persuasive letter.

UNIT 4 Money • **Lesson I** *A New Coat for Anna*

▶ **Writing a Persuasive Letter**

Use a graphic organizer to organize your ideas before you begin writing. One type of graphic organizer is a web. Use the web to plan what you will put in the body of your letter.

☐ Put what you want your audience to do in the circle.

☐ Put facts, reasons, or feelings to convince your reader on the lines surrounding the circle.

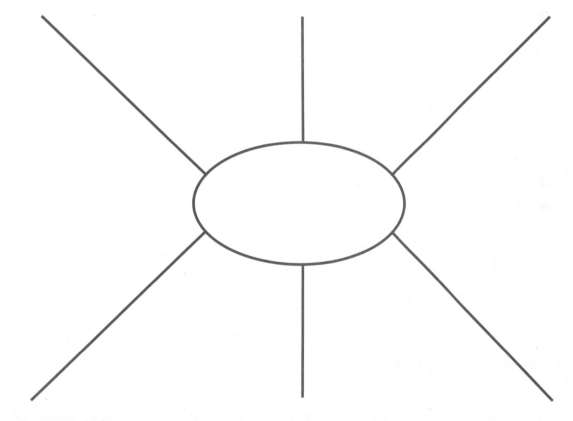

Drafting

Write or type your first draft and put it in your Writing Folder.

Objective: Students prewrite and draft a persuasive letter.

PERSUASIVE WRITING

UNIT 4 Money • **Lesson I** *A New Coat for Anna*

Objective: Students revise a persuasive letter.

▶ Writing a Persuasive Letter

Revising

Read the first draft of your persuasive letter. Use the checklist to help you revise your writing. Use proofreading marks to make changes and corrections.

Ideas

☐ Is the main idea clear?

☐ Do my reasons, facts, or feelings support the action I want my reader to take?

Organization

☐ Did I include all of the ideas from my web?

☐ Does my topic sentence tell my reader what I want?

Word Choice

☐ Did I use the best words to persuade?

☐ Are there any words that I have used too often?

Sentence Fluency

☐ Did I use some short and some long sentences?

Voice

☐ Did I give facts, reasons, or feelings that I care about and that my reader will care about?

If the revised draft of your persuasive friendly letter has many changes, write or type your revision and put it in your Writing Folder.

Proofreading Marks

¶	Indent.
∧	Add something.
≡	Make a capital letter.
sp	Check spelling.
⊙	Add a period.

▶ **Writing a Persuasive Letter**

Editing/Proofreading

Edit your persuasive letter on paper or a computer. Then make a clean copy of your letter, and put it in your Writing Folder. Read your persuasive letter carefully. Use the checklist to help you correct any mistakes.

Conventions

☐ Are your words spelled correctly?

☐ Do you use a capital letter correctly in your heading, greeting, closing, and signature?

☐ Do you use commas correctly?

☐ Does every sentence have a punctuation mark at the end?

☐ Do you indent your paragraphs?

Publishing

Use this checklist to get your letter ready to mail.

Presentation

☐ Make sure your writing says exactly what you want it to say.

☐ Make a clean copy. Make sure you have all the parts of a friendly letter in the correct place. You may want to use the computer.

☐ Address the envelope and send the letter.

Objective: Students edit/proofread and publish a persuasive letter.

PERSUASIVE WRITING

Writing a Persuasive Poster

Objective: Students learn how to create a persuasive poster.

Use the writing process to create a persuasive poster.

Prewriting

Who is the audience for your persuasive poster?

☐ your teacher

☐ your friend

☐ your parent

☐ other _____

What is your purpose for writing the poster?

☐ to persuade someone to buy something

☐ to persuade someone to go to an event

☐ to persuade someone to help with a special project

☐ other _____

Write down colors you would like to use and pictures you would like to include in your poster.

_____

_____

▶ **Writing a Persuasive Poster**

**Organize your ideas before you begin writing.
Write down what you will include on your poster.**

☐ Write the message you want your poster to give your audience in the center square.

☐ List reasons you might use in the surrounding squares.

☐ You may write art to include and colors and types of lettering you want to use in other squares.

Poster Web

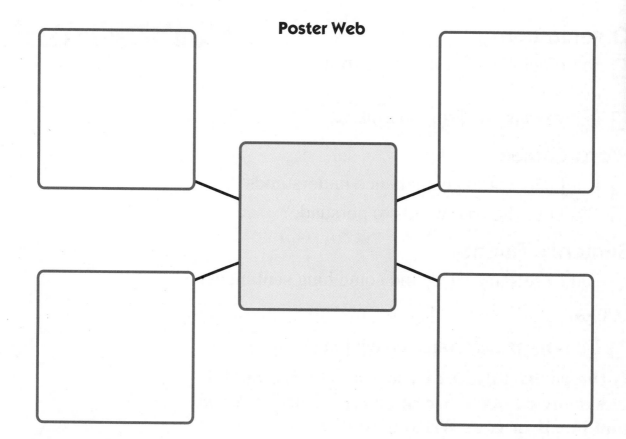

Drafting

**Write or type your first draft and put it in your
Writing Folder.**

Objective: Students prewrite and draft a persuasive poster.

P E R S U A S I V E   W R I T I N G

UNIT 4 Money • **Lesson 2** *Alexander, Who Used to Be Rich Last Sunday*

Objective: Students revise a persuasive poster.

▶ **Writing a Persuasive Poster**

Revising

Read the first draft of your persuasive poster. Use this checklist to revise it. Use editing and proofreading marks to make changes and corrections.

Ideas

☐ Is the main idea clear?

☐ Will my audience care about my message?

Organization

☐ Did I include all of my ideas from prewriting?

☐ Is my poster pleasing to look at?

Word Choice

☐ Did I use words my audience understands?

☐ Did I use the best words to persuade?

Sentence Fluency

☐ Did I use some short and some long sentences?

Voice

☐ Does my poster sound convincing?

If the revised draft of your persuasive poster has many changes, write or type your revision and put it in your Writing Folder.

Proofreading Marks

∧	Add something.
ℓ	Take out something.
≡	Make a capital letter.
sp ⟠	Check spelling.
⊙	Add a period.

Objective: Students edit/proofread and publish a persuasive poster.

PERSUASIVE WRITING

▶ **Writing a Persuasive Poster**

Editing/Proofreading

Edit your persuasive poster on paper or a computer. Then make a clean copy of your letter, and put it in your Writing Folder. Read your persuasive poster carefully. Use the checklist to help you correct any mistakes.

Conventions

☐ Make sure your words are spelled correctly.

☐ Make sure every sentence has a subject and a predicate.

☐ Make sure your subject and predicate agree in number.

☐ Make sure every sentence has a punctuation mark at the end.

Publishing

Use this checklist to make your poster ready to be seen.

Presentation

☐ Make sure your writing says exactly what you want it to say.

☐ Make a clean copy. You may want to use the computer.

☐ Add drawings or pictures to make your poster more appealing.

Name _____ Date _____

Writing a Persuasive Business Letter

Use the writing process to write a persuasive business letter.

Prewriting

Who is the audience for your persuasive business letter?

☐ your teacher

☐ your principal

☐ the president of a company

☐ other _____

What is your purpose for writing this letter?

☐ to persuade a company to sell a new product

☐ to persuade someone to help you or your organization

☐ to persuade a speaker to come to your school or group meeting

☐ other _____

Write the name and address of the person to whom you will send your letter:

Name: _____

Address: _____

City: _____ State: _____ Zip Code: _____

Objective: Students learn how to write a persuasive business letter.

UNIT 4 Money • **Lesson 3** *Kids Did It! In Business*

▶ **Writing a Persuasive Business Letter**

PERSUASIVE WRITING

Objective: Students prewrite and draft a persuasive business letter.

Use a web to write down what reasons, facts, or feelings you will include in the body of your letter.

☐ Tell your reader exactly what it is you want in the circle.

☐ Give facts, reasons, or feelings to support your position on the lines surrounding the circle.

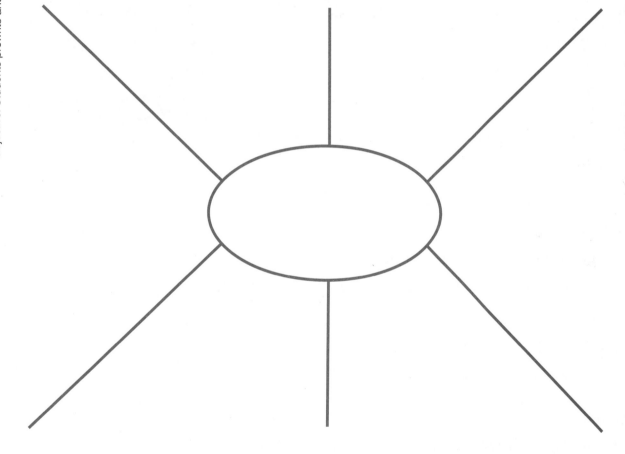

Drafting

Write or type the first draft of your letter and put it in your Writing Folder.

▶ **Writing a Persuasive Business Letter**

Objective: Students revise a persuasive business letter.

Revising

Read the first draft of your business letter. Use this checklist to revise it. Use editing and proofreading marks to make changes and corrections.

Ideas

☐ Do my reasons, facts, and feelings support my main idea?

☐ Are my reasons or facts accurate?

Organization

☐ Do I have all the parts of a business letter in place?

☐ Did I stay on topic?

Word Choice

☐ Did I use words that sound serious?

☐ Did I use words that are polite and respectful?

Sentence Fluency

☐ Have I combined some short sentences to make longer ones?

Voice

☐ Can my reader tell that I am serious about what I'm asking for?

If the revised draft of your persuasive business letter has many changes, write or type your revision and put it in your Writing Folder.

Proofreading Marks	
∧	Add something.
ℓ	Take out something.
≡	Make a capital letter.
sp ⌒	Check spelling.
⊙	Add a period.

> **Writing a Persuasive Business Letter**

PERSUASIVE WRITING

Objective: Students edit/proofread and publish a persuasive business letter.

Editing/Proofreading

Edit your persuasive business letter on paper or a computer. Then make a clean copy of your letter and put it in your Writing Folder. Read your persuasive business letter carefully. Use the checklist to help you correct any mistakes.

Conventions

☐ Have I used periods correctly in abbreviations, initials, and titles?

☐ Have I spelled the name and address of the person to whom I am writing correctly?

☐ Is my grammar businesslike or does it sound like I'm talking to a friend?

Publishing

Use the checklist to get your letter ready to send.

Presentation

☐ Make sure your writing says exactly what you want it to say.

☐ Make sure you have included all the parts of a business letter.

☐ Make a clean copy. You may want to use the computer.

☐ Address the envelope and send your letter.

Writing a Persuasive Paragraph

Objective: Students learn how to write a persuasive paragraph.

Use the writing process to write a persuasive paragraph.

Prewriting

Who is the audience for your persuasive paragraph?

☐ your teacher

☐ a friend

☐ a character in a book

☐ your parent

☐ other _____

What is your purpose for writing this persuasive paragraph?

☐ to persuade someone it is better to be happy than rich

☐ to persuade someone that helping others is a good thing

☐ to persuade someone to give time or money for a good cause

☐ other _____

Write some of the reasons, facts, or feelings you will use in your persuasive paragraph.

_____

_____

UNIT 4   Money • **Lesson 4**   *The Cobbler's Song*

▶ Writing a Persuasive Paragraph

Objective: Students prewrite and draft a persuasive paragraph.

Fill in the web below for your persuasive paragraph.

☐ Put your main idea in the circle.

☐ List one reason, fact, or feeling on each of the lines surrounding the circle.

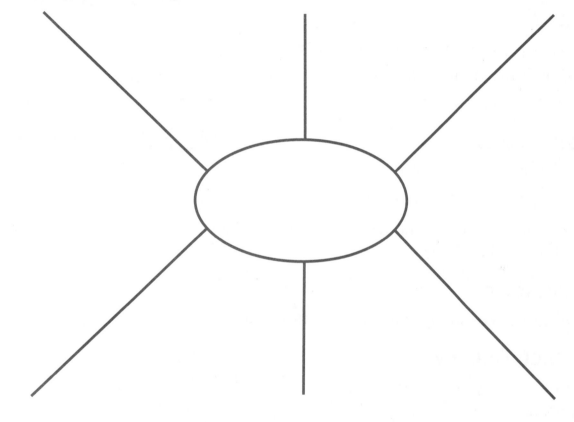

Drafting

Write or type the first draft of your persuasive paragraph and put it in your Writing Folder.

PERSUASIVE WRITING

UNIT 4 Money • **Lesson 4** *The Cobbler's Song*

Objective: Students revise a persuasive paragraph.

▶ **Writing a Persuasive Paragraph**

Revising

Read the first draft of your persuasive paragraph. Use the checklist to revise it. Use editing and proofreading marks to make changes and corrections.

Proofreading Marks

¶	Indent.
∧	Add something.
℮	Take out something.
/	Make a small letter.
sp ◯	Check spelling.

Ideas

☐ Do my reasons, facts, and feelings support my main idea?

☐ Are my reasons or facts accurate?

Organization

☐ Do I have a good topic sentence?

☐ Do my facts or feelings support my main idea?

☐ Did I put the most important fact or strongest feeling in the closing sentence?

Word Choice

☐ Did I use words my reader will understand?

Sentence Fluency

☐ Did I use a good mixture of short and long sentences?

☐ Do I have information in my sentences that is repeated?

Voice

☐ Do I sound as though I'm speaking to my reader?

If the revised draft of your persuasive paragraph has many changes, write or type your revision and put it in your **Writing Folder**.

PERSUASIVE WRITING

▶ **Writing a Persuasive Paragraph**

Editing/Proofreading

Edit your persuasive paragraph on paper or a computer. Then make a clean copy of your paragraph and put it in your Writing Folder. Read your persuasive paragraph carefully. Use the checklist to help you correct any mistakes.

Conventions

- ☐ Have I added *-s* or *-es* correctly?
- ☐ Did I spell possessive nouns correctly?
- ☐ Is it clear which nouns my pronouns replace?
- ☐ Did I use end punctuation correctly?
- ☐ Did I capitalize all proper nouns and the first word of every sentence?

Objective: Students edit/proofread and publish a persuasive paragraph.

Publishing

Use this checklist to get your persuasive paragraph ready for your reader.

Presentation

- ☐ Make sure your writing says exactly what you want it to say.
- ☐ Make a clean copy. You may want to use the computer.
- ☐ Practice reading your persuasive paragraph out loud if you plan to give an oral presentation.

UNIT 4 Money • **Lesson 5** *Four Dollars and Fifty Cents*

Writing a Persuasive Friendly Letter

Use the writing process to write a persuasive friendly letter.

Prewriting

Who is the audience for your persuasive friendly letter?

☐ your teacher

☐ your principal

☐ your parent

☐ other _____

What is your purpose for writing this letter?

☐ to persuade your reader to do what you consider the right thing

☐ to persuade your reader to help you in some way

☐ to persuade your reader to change his or her mind about something

☐ other _____

Write the name and address of the person to whom you will send your letter:

Name: _____

Address: _____

_____

UNIT 4 Money • **Lesson 5** *Four Dollars and Fifty Cents*

▶ **Writing a Persuasive Friendly Letter**

Objective: Students prewrite and draft a persuasive friendly letter.

Use a graphic organizer such as the one below to help you organize your ideas before you begin writing.

☐ Write what you want your reader to do in the circle.

☐ List a reason or fact on each line.

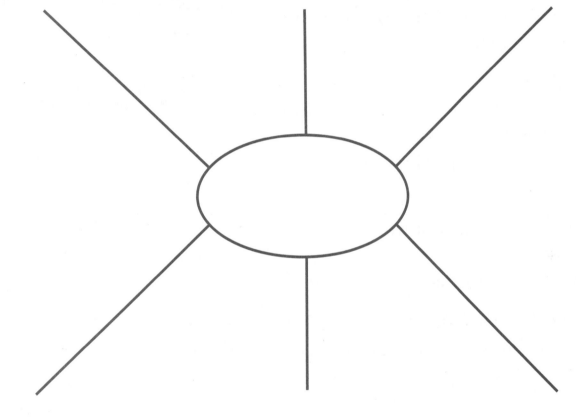

Drafting

Write or type the first draft of your friendly letter and put it in your Writing Folder.

PERSUASIVE WRITING

Name _____ Date _____

▶ **Writing a Persuasive Friendly Letter**

Revising

Read the first draft of your persuasive friendly letter. Use this checklist to revise it. Use editing and proofreading marks to make changes and corrections.

Ideas

☐ Do my reasons or facts support what I want my reader to do?

Organization

☐ Do I have all the parts of a friendly letter in the right places?

☐ Are my paragraphs in the correct order?

Word Choice

☐ Have I used the best words to persuade my reader?

☐ Did I use the same words over and over?

Sentence Fluency

☐ Is there information that can be combined in one sentence?

Voice

☐ Will my reader care about my topic?

If the revised draft of your persuasive friendly letter has many changes, write or type your revision and put it in your Writing Folder.

Proofreading Marks

¶	Indent.
∧	Add something.
ℯ	Take out something.
sp	Check spelling.
⊙	Add a period.

> **Writing a Persuasive Friendly Letter**

Objective: Students edit/proofread and publish a persuasive friendly letter.

PERSUASIVE WRITING

Editing/Proofreading

Edit your persuasive friendly letter on paper or a computer. Then make a clean copy of your letter and put it in your Writing Folder. Read your persuasive friendly letter carefully. Use the checklist to help you correct any mistakes.

Conventions

☐ Do my subjects and verbs agree in number?

☐ Did I use the same tense for my verbs throughout the letter?

☐ Did I use the correct punctuation?

☐ Did I use capital letters correctly?

Publishing

Use this checklist to get your letter ready to send.

Presentation

☐ Make sure your writing says exactly what you want it to say.

☐ Make a clean copy. You may want to use the computer.

☐ Address the envelope and send your letter.

Writing a Persuasive Poster

Objective: Students learn how to create a persuasive poster.

Use the writing process to create a persuasive poster.

Prewriting

Who is the audience for your persuasive poster?

☐ your teacher

☐ your classmates

☐ people in your town

☐ other _____

What is your purpose for writing the poster?

☐ to persuade your reader to buy a raffle ticket

☐ to persuade your reader to support changing the president on a dollar bill

☐ to persuade your reader to donate money for a special project

☐ other _____

Write catch words and phrases that you will use to get your reader's attention:

_____

_____

UNIT 4 Money • **Lesson 6** *The Go-Around Dollar*

▶ **Writing a Persuasive Poster**

Objective: Students prewrite and draft a persuasive poster.

Use a graphic organizer like the web below to organize your thoughts before you begin to create your poster.

☐ Write the message you want your poster to give your audience in the circle.

☐ List phrases, words, and ideas you might use to persuade your readers on the lines surrounding the circle.

☐ Write ideas for art, colors, and lettering on the lines surrounding the circle.

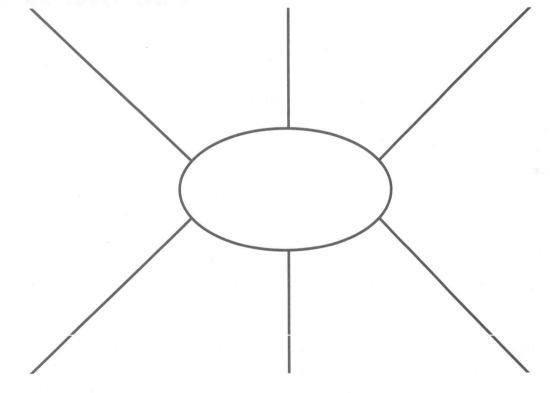

Drafting

Create the first draft of your poster and put it in your Writing Folder.

PERSUASIVE WRITING

Objective: Students revise a persuasive poster.

UNIT 4 Money • **Lesson 6** *The Go-Around Dollar*

Revising

Writing a Persuasive Poster

Look at the first draft of your poster. Use the checklist to revise it. Use editing and proofreading marks to make changes and corrections.

Ideas

☐ Have I presented my idea in a new way?

☐ Did I capture my reader's interest?

☐ Did I give all the important information?

Organization

☐ Does my poster have a focal point that gets my reader's attention?

☐ Did I use the right pictures or drawings for my subject?

Word Choice

☐ Do my words create a picture for the reader?

☐ Did I avoid repeating words?

Sentence Fluency

☐ Are my sentences or phrases easy to read?

Voice

☐ Can my audience feel my excitement in the poster?

If the revised draft of your persuasive poster has many changes, write or type your revision and put it in your Writing Folder.

Proofreading Marks

∧	Add something.
ℓ	Take out something.
≡	Make a capital letter.
sp	Check spelling.

UNIT 4 Money • **Lesson 6** *The Go-Around Dollar*

> **Writing a Persuasive Poster**

Editing/Proofreading

Edit your persuasive poster on paper or a computer. Then make a clean copy of your letter, and put it in your Writing Folder. Read your persuasive poster carefully. Use the checklist to help you correct any mistakes.

Conventions

☐ Make sure your words are spelled correctly.

☐ Make sure you have used adverbs correctly.

☐ Make sure all sentences have end punctuation.

Publishing

Use this checklist to get your poster ready to show others.

Presentation

☐ Make sure your writing says exactly what you want it to say.

☐ Make a clean copy. You may want to use the computer.

☐ Add drawings or pictures to make your poster more appealing.

Objective: Students edit/proofread and publish a persuasive poster.

PERSUASIVE WRITING

Writing a Persuasive Paragraph

Use the writing process to write a persuasive paragraph.

Prewriting

Who is the audience for your persuasive paragraph?

☐ your teacher

☐ a business owner

☐ your older brother or sister

☐ other _____

What is your purpose for writing this paragraph?

☐ to persuade your reader to donate something

☐ to persuade your reader to buy something from you

☐ to persuade your reader to give you an allowance

☐ other _____

Write some of the reasons, facts, or feelings you will use in your persuasive paragraph.

_____

_____

Objective: Students learn how to write a persuasive paragraph.

UNIT 4 Money • **Lesson 7** *Uncle Jed's Barbershop*

Writing a Persuasive Paragraph

Use the graphic organizer below, or create one of your own, to help you organize your thoughts before you begin writing.

☐ Write your main idea in the circle.

☐ Put a reason, fact, or feeling on each line.

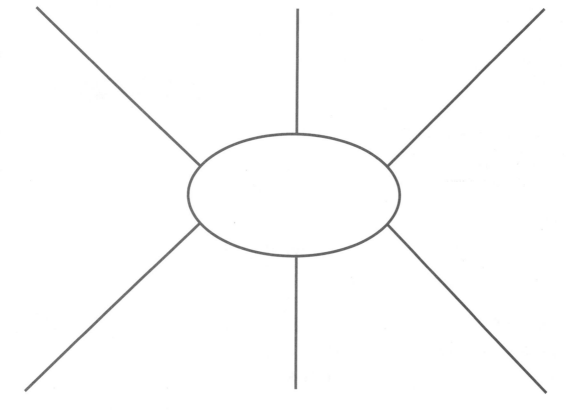

Drafting

Write the first draft of your persuasive paragraph and put it in your Writing Folder.

Objective: Students prewrite and draft a persuasive paragraph.

PERSUASIVE WRITING

Revising

> ▶ **Writing a Persuasive Paragraph**

Read the first draft of your persuasive paragraph. Use this checklist to revise it. Use editing and proofreading marks to make changes and corrections.

Ideas

☐ Do my reasons, facts, and feelings support my main idea?

☐ Are my reasons or facts accurate?

Organization

☐ Do I have a good beginning and ending?

☐ Did I stick to facts or feelings that support my main idea?

Word Choice

☐ Did I choose the best words to say what I feel?

☐ Did I repeat any words too often?

Sentence Fluency

☐ Do my sentences flow smoothly?

☐ Did I use some short and some long sentences?

Voice

☐ Can my reader tell that I feel strongly about my topic?

If the revised draft of your persuasive paragraph has many changes, write or type your revision and put it in your Writing Folder.

Proofreading Marks	
¶	Indent.
∧	Add something.
ℯ	Take out something.
⌢sp	Check spelling.
⊙	Add a period.

Objective: Students revise a persuasive paragraph.

PERSUASIVE WRITING

Writing a Persuasive Paragraph

Editing/Proofreading

Objective: Students edit/proofread and publish a persuasive paragraph.

Edit your persuasive paragraph on paper or a computer. Then make a clean copy of your paragraph, and put it in your Writing Folder. Read your persuasive paragraph carefully. Use the checklist to help you correct any mistakes.

Conventions

☐ Does every sentence have a subject and a predicate?

☐ Did I use pronouns and adverbs correctly?

☐ Does every sentence have end punctuation?

☐ Did I capitalize all proper nouns and the first word of every sentence?

☐ Is my paragraph indented?

☐ Are the words spelled correctly?

Publishing

Use the checklist to get your persuasive paragraph ready for your reader.

Presentation

☐ Make sure your writing says exactly what you want it to say.

☐ Make a clean copy. You may want to use the computer.

☐ Practice reading your persuasive paragraph out loud if you plan to give an oral presentation.

Writing a Fantasy

Objective: Students learn how to write a fantasy.

Use the writing process to write a fantasy story.

Prewriting

Who is the audience for your fantasy?

☐ your classmates

☐ your teacher

☐ your friends

☐ other _____

What is your purpose for writing this fantasy?

☐ to tell about an animal with special powers

☐ to tell about a place that only children can understand

☐ to tell about a person who is from a different world

☐ other _____

What special powers or place will your main character have or come from?

_____

UNIT 5 Storytelling • **Lesson I** *A Story, A Story*

Writing a Fantasy

Use a graphic organizer to help you organize your thoughts before you begin writing. A good graphic organizer to use for a fantasy is a character web.

☐ Put your main character's name or type of being in the center oval.

☐ Write the special powers that the main character has on the surrounding lines.

Character Web

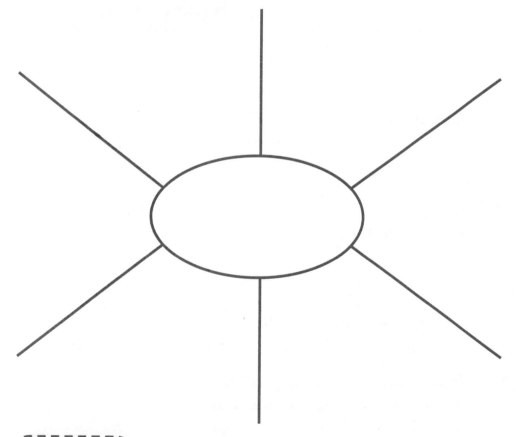

Objective: Students prewrite and draft a fantasy.

NARRATIVE WRITING

Drafting

Write the first draft of your fantasy story on notebook paper or on a computer and put it in your Writing Folder.

UNIT 5 Storytelling • **Lesson I** *A Story, A Story*

> Writing a Fantasy

Objective: Students learn how to revise a fantasy.

Revising

Read the first draft of your fantasy. Use the checklist to help you revise. Use editing and proofreading marks to make changes and corrections.

Ideas

☐ Do you describe the setting so your readers feel as if they are there?

Organization

☐ Did you include all of your ideas from prewriting?

Word Choice

☐ Do your words help the readers realize there is something unreal about the characters, setting, or events?

Sentence Fluency

☐ Have you used some long and some short sentences?

Voice

☐ Can your readers hear you telling the story to them?

If the revised draft of your fantasy has many changes, write or type your revisions and put them in your Writing Folder. If you typed your draft on a computer, you can use the cut, copy, and paste buttons on the toolbar to move words, sentences, and paragraphs.

Proofreading Marks

¶	Indent.
∧	Add something.
≡	Make a capital letter.
⟋sp	Check spelling.
⊙	Add a period.

▶ **Writing a Fantasy**

Editing/Proofreading

Edit/proofread your fantasy on notebook paper or on a computer and put it in your Writing Folder. Read your fantasy carefully. Use the checklist to help you correct any mistakes. Make your writing easy to read and understand.

Conventions

☐ Are all of your words spelled correctly?

☐ Do you have a capital letter at the beginning of each sentence and proper noun?

☐ Do you correctly use commas in compound sentences?

☐ Does every sentence have a punctuation mark at the end?

☐ Are your paragraphs indented?

Publishing

Use the checklist to get your fantasy story ready for your readers.

Presentation

☐ Write or type a neat final copy of your fantasy.

☐ Make sure you have added all the changes you made during revising and editing.

☐ Illustrate your story.

☐ Bind it in a book.

Objective: Students edit, proofread, and publish a fantasy.

NARRATIVE WRITING

Objective: Students learn how to write a biography.

UNIT 5 Storytelling • **Lesson 2** *Oral History*

Writing a Biography

Use the writing process to write a biography.

Prewriting

Who is the audience for your biography?

☐ your teacher

☐ your classmates

☐ the subject of your biography

☐ other _____

What is your purpose for writing the biography?

☐ to tell about a famous person

☐ to tell about a person whose works or deeds you admire

☐ to tell about a person who is important in your life

☐ other _____

Who is the subject of your biography?

_____

UNIT 5 Storytelling • **Lesson 2** *Oral History*

▶ **Writing a Biography**

NARRATIVE WRITING

Objective: Students prewrite and draft a biography.

Use a graphic organizer to help you organize your thoughts before you begin writing. A good graphic organizer to use for a biography is a time line.

☐ Write important events in the person's life below the line.

☐ Write the dates that go with each event on top of the line.

☐ Often the dates of birth and death are included. Other important events are added in between.

Time Line

Date:

Event:

Drafting

Create the first draft of your biography on notebook paper or on a computer and put it in your Writing Folder.

Name _____ Date _____

▶ **Writing a Biography**

Revising

Read the first draft of your biography. Use the checklist to help you revise. Use editing and proofreading marks to make changes and corrections.

Ideas

☐ Is the subject of your biography clear?

☐ Do your details tell more about your subject?

Organization

☐ Are your events in the correct time order?

☐ Do you stay on topic in each paragraph?

Word Choice

☐ Do you use descriptive words to tell about the person and events?

Sentence Fluency

☐ Do you use a variety of sentences?

Voice

☐ Does your interest in your topic come across in your biography?

If the revised draft of your biography has many changes, write or type your revisions and put them in your Writing Folder. If you typed your draft on a computer, you can use the cut, copy, and paste buttons on the toolbar to move words, sentences, and paragraphs.

Proofreading Marks	
	Indent.
	Add something.
	Take out something.
	Make a capital letter.
	Check spelling.

Objective: Students revise a biography.

▶ **Writing a Biography**

Objective: Students edit, proofread, and publish a biography.

NARRATIVE WRITING

Editing/Proofreading

Edit/proofread your biography on notebook paper or on a computer and put it in your Writing Folder. Read your biography carefully. Use the checklist to help you correct any mistakes. Make your writing easy to read and understand.

Conventions

☐ Make sure that all names are spelled and capitalized correctly.

☐ Make sure that every sentence has a subject and a predicate.

☐ Make sure that you have used commas in dates correctly.

☐ Make sure that every sentence has a punctuation mark at the end.

Publishing

Use the checklist to get your biography ready to share.

Presentation

☐ Write or type a clean copy of your biography.

☐ Make all of the corrections you marked during revising and editing.

☐ Add photographs or illustrations with captions.

Writing a Personal Narrative

Objective: Students learn how to write a personal narrative.

Use the writing process to write a personal narrative.

Prewriting

Who is the audience for your personal narrative?

☐ your parents

☐ your teacher

☐ your pen pal

☐ other _____

What is your purpose for writing the personal narrative?

☐ to tell about an important event in your life

☐ to tell about something fun you did

☐ to tell about a funny thing that happened to you

☐ other _____

What event in your life will you use for your personal narrative?

_____

Name _____   Date _____

Objective: Students prewrite and draft a personal narrative.

NARRATIVE WRITING

▶ **Writing a Personal Narrative**

A good graphic organizer to use for a personal narrative is a chain-of-events graphic organizer.

☐ Write what happened first in the top box.

☐ Follow the arrows and fill in the rest of the boxes in the order that things happened next.

Chain of Events

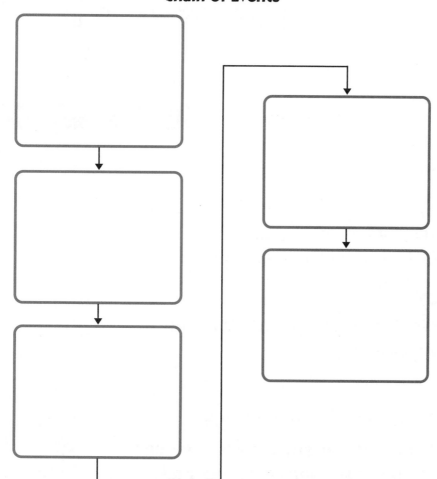

Drafting

Write or type the first draft of your personal narrative and put it in your Writing Folder.

► **Writing a Personal Narrative**

Revising

Read the first draft of your personal narrative. Use the checklist to help you revise. Use editing and proofreading marks to make changes and corrections.

Proofreading Marks

¶	Indent.
∧	Add something.
ℓ	Take out something.
/	Make a small letter.
sp	Check spelling.

Ideas

☐ Is the event you chose meaningful to you?

Organization

☐ Do you include everything from your graphic organizer?

☐ Does your beginning grab the reader?

Word Choice

☐ Do you use words that help your reader see, hear, smell, taste, or feel what you are describing?

Sentence Fluency

☐ Do your sentences sound like the ones that you use when you are speaking?

Voice

☐ Can your reader tell what you were feeling?

If the revised draft of your personal narrative has many changes, write or type your revisions and put them in your Writing Folder. If you typed your draft on a computer, you can use the cut, copy, and paste buttons on the toolbar to move words, sentences, and paragraphs.

Objective: Students revise a personal narrative.

Objective: Students edit, proofread, and publish a personal narrative.

► **Writing a Personal Narrative**

Editing/Proofreading

Edit/proofread your personal narrative on notebook paper or on a computer and put it in your Writing Folder. Read your narrative carefully. Use the checklist to help you correct any mistakes. Make your writing easy to read and understand.

Conventions

☐ Do you spell everything correctly?

☐ Do you use commas and exclamation points correctly?

☐ Do you indent your paragraphs?

☐ Do you have any run-on sentences?

Publishing

Use the checklist to get your personal narrative ready to share with your reader.

Presentation

☐ Write or type a neat final copy of your personal narrative.

☐ Make sure that you make all the editing/ proofreading changes you marked.

☐ Add illustrations or photographs.

NARRATIVE WRITING

Objective: Students learn how to write a realistic story.

UNIT 5 Storytelling • **Lesson 4** *Carving the Pole*

Writing a Realistic Story

Use the writing process to write a realistic story.

Prewriting

Who is the audience for your realistic story?

☐ your brother or sister

☐ your classmates

☐ your teacher

☐ other _____

What is your purpose for writing the realistic story?

☐ to tell about a time that someone learned a lesson

☐ to tell about a very special present

☐ to tell about a time when a person or animal helped someone

☐ other _____

UNIT 5 Storytelling • **Lesson 4** *Carving the Pole*

▶ **Writing a Realistic Story**

Objective: Students prewrite and draft a realistic story.

A good graphic organizer to use for a realistic story is a story map.

- Write what happens first in your realistic story in the beginning box.
- Write the body of your story in the middle box.
- Write the ending to your story in the end box.

Story Map

Beginning

_____

Middle

_____

_____

_____

End

_____

Drafting

Write a first draft of your realistic story in your Writing Folder. Remember to include all of your ideas from prewriting.

NARRATIVE WRITING

UNIT 5 Storytelling • **Lesson 4** *Carving the Pole*

Objective: Students revise a realistic story.

▶ **Writing a Realistic Story**

Revising

Read the first draft of your realistic story. Use the checklist to help you revise. Use editing and proofreading marks to make changes and corrections.

Ideas

☐ Do you make sure that your characters, setting, and events could be real?

☐ Do you give your reader something new to read about?

Organization

☐ Does the beginning get the reader interested right away?

☐ Are your events in an order that makes sense?

Word Choice

☐ Have you given your characters personalities with the words you have used?

Sentence Fluency

☐ Do you use dialogue to keep things flowing?

Voice

☐ Does it sound as though you wrote to your audience?

If the revised draft of your realistic story has many changes, write or type your revisions and put them in your Writing Folder.

Proofreading Marks	
ℿ	Indent.
∧	Add something.
ℓ	Take out something.
sp⊙	Check spelling.
⊙	Add a period.

▶ **Writing a Realistic Story**

Objective: Students edit, proofread, and publish a realistic story.

Editing/Proofreading

Edit/proofread your realistic story on notebook paper or on a computer and put it in your Writing Folder. Read your story carefully. Use the checklist to help you correct any mistakes. Make your writing easy to read and understand.

Conventions

☐ Have you spelled everything correctly?

☐ Have you used capital letters, quotation marks, and commas correctly in dialogue?

☐ Is it clear who is speaking when you use dialogue?

☐ Do you have any rambling or run-on sentences?

Publishing

Use the checklist to get your realistic story ready to share with your readers.

Presentation

☐ Write or type a clean copy of your realistic story.

☐ Make all of the changes you marked during revising and editing.

☐ Give your story a title.

NARRATIVE WRITING

Writing a Mystery

Objective: Students learn how to write a mystery.

Use the writing process to write a mystery.

Prewriting

Who is the audience for your mystery?

☐ your parents

☐ your friend

☐ your classmates

☐ your teacher

☐ other _____

What is your purpose for writing the mystery?

☐ to tell about something that suddenly disappeared

☐ to tell about someone who was acting strangely

☐ to tell about something that happened in a town
long ago

☐ other _____

UNIT 5 Storytelling • **Lesson 5** *The Keeping Quilt*

▶ **Writing a Mystery**

NARRATIVE WRITING

Objective: Students prewrite and draft a mystery.

A good graphic organizer to use for a mystery is a story map.

- Write what happens first in your mystery in the beginning box.
- Write the body of your mystery in the middle box.
- Write the ending to your mystery in the end box.

Story Map

Beginning
_____

Middle
_____
_____
_____

End
_____

Drafting

Write or type the first draft of your mystery and put it in your Writing Folder.

UNIT 5 Storytelling • **Lesson 5** *The Keeping Quilt*

▶ **Writing a Mystery**

Objective: Students revise a mystery.

Revising

Read the first draft of your mystery. Use the checklist to help you revise. Use editing and proofreading marks to make changes and corrections.

Ideas

☐ Do you have a clear problem?

☐ Do you use details to give a clear picture of characters and setting?

Organization

☐ Do your clues lead to the solution?

☐ Does your ending make sense?

Word Choice

☐ Did you use words that add to the suspense and surprise?

Sentence Fluency

☐ Do all of your sentences begin the same?

Voice

☐ Does the personality of the person solving the mystery come through?

If the revised draft of your mystery has many changes, write or type your revisions and put them in your Writing Folder.

Proofreading Marks

¶	Indent.
∧	Add something.
ℓ	Take out something.
sp ◯	Check spelling.
⊙	Add a period.

► **Writing a Mystery**

NARRATIVE WRITING

Objective: Students edit, proofread, and publish a mystery.

Editing/Proofreading

Edit/proofread your mystery on notebook paper or on a computer and put it in your Writing Folder. Read your mystery carefully. Use the checklist to help you correct any mistakes. Make your writing easy to read and understand.

Conventions

☐ Did you capitalize proper nouns, the pronoun *I*, and any initials correctly?

☐ Did you use periods correctly?

☐ Did you indent each paragraph?

☐ Did you punctuate dialogue correctly?

☐ Is it clear which nouns the pronouns replace?

Publishing

Use the checklist to get your mystery ready to share.

Presentation

☐ Write or type a clean copy of your mystery.

☐ Add illustrations and a title.

☐ Send your story to a newspaper or children's magazine to be published.

Objective: Students learn how to write a tall tale.

UNIT 5 Storytelling • **Lesson 6** *Johnny Appleseed*

Writing a Tall Tale

Use the writing process to create a tall tale.

Prewriting

Who is the audience for your tall tale?

☐ a classmate

☐ your teacher

☐ your cousin

☐ other _____

What is your purpose for writing the tall tale?

☐ to tell about a historical figure

☐ to tell about a character you have made up

☐ to change a personal narrative or realistic fiction
   into a tall tale

☐ other _____

UNIT 5 Storytelling • **Lesson 6** *Johnny Appleseed*

NARRATIVE WRITING

Objective: Students prewrite and draft a tall tale.

Use a graphic organizer to help you organize your thoughts before you begin writing. A good graphic organizer to use for a tall tale is a character web.

☐ Put the name of your main character in the center oval.

☐ Write exaggerated things that the main character does on the surrounding lines.

Character Web

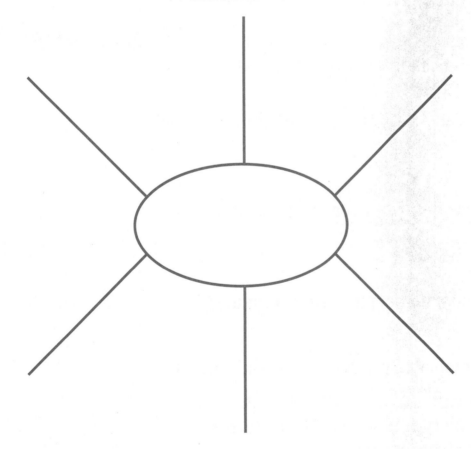

Drafting

Write or type the first draft of your tall tale and put it in your Writing Folder.

UNIT 5 Storytelling • **Lesson 6** *Johnny Appleseed*

Revising

Read the first draft of your tall tale. Use the checklist to help you revise. Use editing and proofreading marks to make changes and corrections.

Ideas

☐ Do you use exaggeration?

☐ Do your details give a clear picture of characters, setting, and plot?

Organization

☐ Are your sentences in an order that makes sense?

☐ Does your creative solution go with your unusual problem?

Word Choice

☐ Do your words help your reader get to know your character?

Sentence Fluency

☐ Does your dialogue keep the story moving?

Voice

☐ Did you remember to put humor in your tall tale?

If the revised draft of your tall tale has many changes, write or type your revisions and put them in your Writing Folder.

Proofreading Marks

¶   Indent.

∧   Add something.

ℓ   Take out something.

≡   Make a capital letter.

sp   Check spelling.

Writing a Tall Tale

NARRATIVE WRITING

Objective: Students edit, proofread, and publish a tall tale.

Editing/Proofreading

Edit/proofread your tall tale on notebook paper or on a computer and put it in your Writing Folder. Read your writing carefully. Use the checklist to help you correct any mistakes. Make your writing easy to read and understand.

Conventions

☐ Do you use quotation marks, commas, and capital letters correctly in dialogue?

☐ Did you capitalize dates, holidays, historic periods, and special events correctly?

Publishing

Use the checklist to get your tall tale ready for your audience.

Presentation

☐ Write or type a neat final copy of your tall tale.

☐ Give your tall tale a title.

☐ Illustrate your tall tale.

☐ Make your tall tale into a book.

Writing a Play

Use the writing process to write a play.

Prewriting

Who is the audience for your play?

☐ a group of children at the library

☐ children and adults at a community theater

☐ your classmates

☐ your family

☐ other _____

What is your purpose for writing the play?

☐ to retell your favorite story

☐ to tell about something you have learned in school

☐ to tell about someone's life

☐ to persuade the audience to do something good
for the community, such as recycling

☐ other _____

Objective: Students learn how to write a play.

▶ **Writing a Play**

NARRATIVE WRITING

Objective: Students prewrite and draft a play.

Use the graphic organizer below to help you organize your thoughts.

☐ Write the names of characters in the top box.

☐ Write down props you will need in the Props box.

☐ Write the setting for your play in the Setting box.

☐ Write ideas for the beginning, middle, and end in the Plot box.

Play Graphic Organizer

Characters

_____ _____ _____

Props

_____ _____ _____

Setting

_____

Plot

Beginning: _____

Middle: _____

End: _____

Drafting

- **Write the first draft of your play or type it on a computer and put it in your Writing Folder.**

Writing a Play

Objective: Students revise a play.

Revising

Read the first draft of your play. Use the checklist to help you revise. Use editing and proofreading marks to make changes and corrections.

Ideas

☐ Do the characters' lines tell the story?

☐ Are your stage directions clear?

Organization

☐ Do the stage directions support what the characters are saying?

☐ Do the characters' lines tell the story in an order that makes sense?

☐ Does your ending wrap up the story?

Word Choice

☐ Do you use precise words in your stage directions?

Sentence Fluency

☐ Do your characters' lines flow?

Voice

☐ Did you keep your audience in mind while you wrote the play?

If the revised draft of your play has many changes, write or type your revisions and put them in your Writing Folder.

Proofreading Marks

∧	Add something.
ℓ	Take out something.
☰	Make a capital letter.
✀	Check spelling.
⊙	Add a period.

▶ **Writing a Play**

Objective: Students edit, proofread, and publish a play.

NARRATIVE WRITING

Editing/Proofreading

Edit/proofread your play on notebook paper or on a computer and put it in your Writing Folder. Read your play carefully. Use the checklist to help you correct any mistakes. Make your writing easy to read and understand.

Conventions

☐ Do you have the characters' names at the beginning of their lines?

☐ Did you spell everything correctly?

☐ Did you put the stage directions in parentheses and underline them?

☐ Did you remember to use punctuation at the end of each sentence?

Publishing

Use this checklist to get your play ready for your audience.

Presentation

☐ Give your play a title.

☐ Write or type a neat final copy of your play.

☐ Put a cover on your final copy.

☐ Make a list of props you will need.

☐ Perform your play.

UNIT 6 Country Life • **Lesson 1** *The Country Mouse and the City Mouse*

Writing a Personal Essay

Use the writing process to write a personal essay.

Prewriting

Who is the audience for your personal essay?

☐ Your teacher

☐ Your friends or classmates

☐ Your family

☐ A younger child

☐ Other _____

What is your purpose for writing this personal essay?

☐ To tell a story about yourself that explains your thoughts or feelings about something

☐ To entertain with a story from your life

☐ Other _____

What event, experience, or activity are you writing about in this personal essay?

_____

Name _____ Date _____

> **Writing a Personal Essay**

Objective: Students prewrite and draft a personal essay.

PERSONAL WRITING

Use the following graphic organizer to help you organize your personal essay.

Story Map

Beginning	What Happened	How I felt
_____		_____

Middle	What Happened	How I felt
_____		_____
_____		_____
_____		_____
_____		_____

End	What Happened	How I felt
_____		_____

Drafting

- Write the first draft of your personal essay or type it on a computer and put it in your Writing Folder.

- Leave space between the lines for changes and corrections.

UNIT 6 Country Life • **Lesson I** *The Country Mouse and the City Mouse*

Objective: Students revise a personal essay.

▶ **Writing a Personal Essay**

Revising

Read the first draft of your personal essay. Use the checklist to help you make your writing better. Use editing and proofreading marks to make changes and corrections.

Ideas

☐ Does your personal essay have a beginning, a middle, and an end?

Organization

☐ Does the order of your paragraphs make your beginning, middle, and end clear?

Word Choice

☐ Did you use time and order words to help your readers follow the action?

☐ Did you use place and location words to let your readers know where people, things, and events are?

Sentence Fluency

☐ Did you make two or more sentences from run-on sentences?

Voice

☐ Read your personal essay out loud. Are your thoughts and feelings about the events in your story obvious?

If your revised draft of your personal essay has many changes, write or type your revision and put it in your Writing Folder.

Proofreading Marks

¶	Indent.
∧	Add something.
ℓ	Take out something.
≡	Make a capital letter.
/	Make a small letter.
sp	Check spelling.
⊙	Add a period.

Writing a Personal Essay

PERSONAL WRITING

Objective: Students edit/proofread and publish a personal essay.

Editing/Proofreading

Edit/proofread your personal essay on notebook paper or on a computer and put it in your Writing Folder. Read your personal essay carefully. Use the checklist to help you correct any mistakes. Make your writing easy to read and understand.

Conventions

☐ Are all the names of people, places, and things spelled correctly? Use a dictionary if you are unsure of the spelling.

☐ Did you use commas in dates, between a city and state or country, and after *yes* and *no?*

☐ Did you use quotation marks for any quotations, and exclamation points for statements with strong feelings?

☐ Did you capitalize the title and any proper nouns in your personal essay?

☐ Are all your paragraphs indented?

Publishing

Use the checklist to get your essay ready to share.

Presentation

☐ Write or type a neat final copy of your personal essay.

☐ Add a drawing, photograph, or computer graphic to add interest.

☐ Practice reading your personal essay out loud if you plan to give an oral presentation.

UNIT 6 Country Life • **Lesson 2** *Heartland*

Writing an Invitation

Objective: Students learn how to write an invitation.

Use the writing process to write an invitation.

Prewriting

Who is the audience for your invitation?

☐ Your teacher

☐ Your friend

☐ Your classmate

☐ Your family

☐ A younger child

☐ Other _____

What is your purpose for writing this invitation?

☐ To ask someone to come to a party

☐ To ask someone to visit your home

☐ To ask your parent to visit your class

☐ Other _____

UNIT 6 Country Life • **Lesson 2** *Heartland*

▶ **Writing an Invitation**

Objective: Students prewrite and draft an invitation.

Use the following graphic organizer or make one of your own to help you organize the information for your invitation.

• On the body lines, write the date, time, place, and the reason for the invitation.

Invitation Graphic Organizer

Date: _____

Time: _____

Place: _____

Reason: _____

Address for Envelope

Drafting

• **Write the first draft of your invitation or type it on a computer and put it in your Writing Folder.**

Objective: Students revise an invitation.

Writing an Invitation

Revising

Read the first draft of your invitation. Use the checklist to help you revise. Use editing and proofreading marks to make changes and corrections.

Ideas

☐ Does your invitation include all the information from your graphic organizer?

☐ Did you include all the parts of an invitation?

Organization

☐ Is the information organized in a way that is easy to understand?

Word Choice

☐ Did you choose words that are clear and specific so that your reader will know exactly what you are asking?

Sentence Fluency

☐ Did you combine short, choppy sentences with conjunctions?

Voice

☐ Does your invitation sound friendly and inviting?

If the revised draft of your invitation has many changes, write out your revision and put it in your Writing Folder.

Proofreading Marks

¶	Indent.
∧	Add something.
	Take out something.
≡	Make a capital letter.
/	Make a small letter.
	Check spelling.
⊙	Add a period.

UNIT 6 Country Life • **Lesson 2** *Heartland*

▶ **Writing an Invitation**

Objective: Students edit/proofread and publish an invitation.

PERSONAL WRITING

Editing/Proofreading

Edit/proofread your invitation on notebook paper or on a computer and put it in your Writing Folder. Read your invitation carefully. Use the checklist to help you correct any mistakes. Make your invitation easy to read and understand.

Conventions

☐ Are all the names of people, places, and dates spelled correctly?

☐ Did you use apostrophes with possessive nouns?

☐ Did you use hyphens to divide words?

☐ If you asked a question, did you end it with a question mark?

Publishing

Use the checklist to get your invitation ready to send.

Presentation

☐ Write or type a neat final copy of your invitation.

☐ Add small drawings, a map, or computer graphics to add interest and information to your invitation.

UNIT 6 Country Life • **Lesson 3** *Leah's Pony*

Writing a Friendly Letter

Use the writing process to write a friendly letter.

Prewriting

Who is the audience for your friendly letter?

☐ Your teacher

☐ Your friend

☐ Your relative

☐ Your pen pal

☐ Other _____

What is your purpose for writing this letter?

☐ To share news, stories, and thoughts

☐ To keep in touch

☐ To start or continue a friendship

☐ Other _____

Name _____ Date _____

> **Writing a Friendly Letter**

Use the following graphic organizer to help you organize your news, stories, and thoughts for a friendly letter.

Objective: Students prewrite and draft a friendly letter.

PERSONAL WRITING

> **Friendly Letter Graphic Organizer**

Heading

_____ Greeting

Topic _____

_____

Details

_____

_____

Closing _____

Signature _____

Address for Envelope

Drafting

• Write the first draft of your friendly letter or type it on a computer and put it in your Writing Folder.

UNIT 6 Country Life • **Lesson 3** *Leah's Pony*

▶ Writing a Friendly Letter

Objective: Students revise a friendly letter.

Revising

Read the first draft of your friendly letter. Use this checklist to help you revise. Use editing and proofreading marks to make changes and corrections.

Ideas

☐ Did you include all of the parts of a friendly letter?

Organization

☐ Is there a topic sentence for each paragraph?

☐ Do all of the sentences in a paragraph tell about the topic of the paragraph?

Word Choice

☐ Did you use the correct main and helping verbs?

☐ Did you add variety by substituting pronouns for nouns?

Sentence Fluency

☐ Did you use different types of sentences to make your writing more interesting to read?

Voice

☐ Does your friendly letter sound like you are talking to a friend?

If the revised draft of your friendly letter has many changes, write or type your revision and put it in your **Writing Folder.**

Proofreading Marks

 Indent.

 Add something.

 Take out something.

 Make a capital letter.

 Make a small letter.

 Check spelling.

⊙ Add a period.

UNIT 6 Country Life • **Lesson 3** *Leah's Pony*

▶ **Writing a Friendly Letter**

Objective: Students edit/proofread and publish a friendly letter.

Editing/Proofreading

Edit/proofread your friendly letter on notebook paper or on a computer and put it in your Writing Folder. Read your letter carefully. Use the checklist to help you correct any mistakes. Make your letter easy to read and understand.

Conventions

☐ Are all the names of people and places spelled correctly?

☐ Did you capitalize the greeting and closing?

☐ Did you capitalize the first word of every sentence?

☐ Did you use exclamation points at the ends of statements with strong feelings?

☐ Did you use question marks at the ends of questions?

Publishing

Use the checklist to help get your letter ready to send.

Presentation

☐ Write or type a neat final copy of your letter.

☐ Add a drawing, map, photograph, or computer graphic to add interest.

PERSONAL WRITING

Writing a Business Letter

Use the writing process to write a business letter.

Prewriting

Who is the audience for your business letter?

☐ Your teacher

☐ Your family

☐ A store owner

☐ Other _____

What is your purpose for writing this business letter?

☐ To request information

☐ To complain about a problem

☐ To state your concern about something that affects many people

☐ Other _____

Objective: Students learn how to write a business letter.

▶ **Writing a Business Letter**

PERSONAL WRITING

Objective: Students prewrite and draft a business letter.

Use the following graphic organizer or make one
of your own to help you organize your thoughts
for your business letter.

Business Letter Graphic Organizer

Heading

Inside Address

_____ Greeting

_____ Body

_____

_____

_____

Closing _____

Signature _____

Drafting

• Write the first draft of your business letter or
type it on a computer and put it in your Writing
Folder.

▶ Writing a Business Letter

Revising

Read the first draft of your business letter. Use the checklist to help you revise. Use editing and proofreading marks to make changes and corrections.

Ideas

☐ Do you stay on the topic?

☐ Did you include all of the parts of a business letter?

Organization

☐ Are your sentences in the order that best makes your purpose clearly understood?

Word Choice

☐ Did you choose words that are serious and polite?

Sentence Fluency

☐ Did you combine short, choppy sentences with conjunctions?

Voice

☐ Does your business letter sound like you are talking to an adult whom you respect?

If the revised draft of your business letter has many changes, write out revisions on notebook paper and put it in your Writing Folder. If you have typed your draft on a computer, you can use the cut, copy, and paste buttons on the toolbar to move around words, sentences, and paragraphs.

Proofreading Marks

∧	Add something.
ℓ	Take out something.
≡	Make a capital letter.
/	Make a small letter.
⊙	Check spelling.
⊙	Add a period.

Objective: Students revise a business letter.

► **Writing a Business Letter**

Editing/Proofreading

Edit/proofread your business letter on notebook paper or on a computer and put it in your Writing Folder. Read your business letter carefully. Use this checklist to help you correct any mistakes. Make your letter easy to read and understand.

Conventions

☐ Are all of the names of people and places spelled correctly?

☐ Did you use question marks at the end of questions?

☐ Did you use quotation marks and commas to punctuate quotations?

☐ Did you use commas when listing three or more things in a series?

☐ Are all the proper nouns capitalized?

☐ Did you capitalize the greeting and the closing?

Publishing

Use the checklist to get your letter ready to send.

Presentation

☐ Write or type a neat final copy of your letter.

☐ Address an envelope.

Name _____ Date _____

Writing a Learning Log

Use the writing process to write a learning log.

Prewriting

Who is the audience for your learning log?

☐ Your teacher

☐ Your classmates

☐ Your family

☐ Other _____

What is your purpose for writing this learning log?

☐ To study a subject by observing and recording data

☐ To inform others about a subject you have been studying

☐ Other _____

What is the subject you are using a learning log to study?

☐ Other _____

Name _____ Date _____

► **Writing a Learning Log**

Use the following graphic organizer or make one of your own to help you organize the data in your learning log.

Objective: Students prewrite and draft a learning log.

PERSONAL WRITING

Learning Log Graphic Organizer

[ ] Date

[ ] Time

[ ] Place

[ ] Subject

_____

_____

Details

_____

Drafting

• Write the first entry of your learning log and put it in your Writing Folder.

Objective: Students revise a learning log.

▶ **Writing a Learning Log**

Revising

Read the first drafts of your log entries. Use the checklist to help you revise. Use editing and proofreading marks to make changes and corrections.

Ideas

☐ Do your entries record changes that happened over a period of time?

☐ Do you explain any drawings or photographs?

Organization

☐ Would the data you collected be easier to understand in a chart or Venn diagram?

Word Choice

☐ Do you use specific adjectives to describe your subject's changes?

☐ Do you use time and order words to help readers know when things happen?

☐ Do you use the correct verb tenses and articles?

Sentence Fluency

☐ Are all of your observations written in complete sentences?

Voice

☐ Does your learning log sound like you liked observing and recording data about your subject?

If the revised draft of your learning log has many changes, write or type it and put it in your Writing Folder.

Proofreading Marks	
∧	Add something.
ℓ	Take out something.
≡	Make a capital letter.
/	Make a small letter.
⌢sp	Check spelling.
⊙	Add a period.

> ▶ Writing a Learning Log

PERSONAL WRITING

Objective: Students edit/proofread and publish a learning log.

Editing/Proofreading

Edit/proofread your learning log on notebook paper or on a computer and put it in your Writing Folder. Read your learning log carefully. Use the checklist to help you correct any mistakes. Make your writing easy to read and understand.

Conventions

☐ Are all contractions and plural nouns spelled correctly?

☐ Did you capitalize the first word of every sentence?

☐ Did you use commas and periods to help make your writing easier to read and understand?

Publishing

Use the checklist to get your learning log ready to share.

Presentation

☐ Write or type a neat final copy of your learning log.

☐ Add drawings, photographs, a chart, or a map to add interest.

☐ Practice reading your learning log out loud if you plan to give an oral presentation.

Writing a Thank-You Note

Objective: Students learn how to write a thank-you note.

Use the writing process to write a thank-you note.

Prewriting

Who is the audience for your thank-you note?

☐ Your teacher

☐ Your classmate

☐ Your friend

☐ Your relative

☐ Other _____

What is your purpose for writing a thank-you note?

☐ To thank your teacher for helping you with a big writing project

☐ To thank your classmate for giving you a birthday present

☐ To thank your relative for letting you visit

☐ Other _____

▶ **Writing a Thank-You Note**

PERSONAL WRITING

Objective: Students prewrite and draft a thank-you note.

Use the following graphic organizer or make one of your own to help you organize your thoughts before writing your thank-you note.

Thank-You Note Graphic Organizer

Greeting

_____ Body

_____

_____

_____

_____

Closing _____

Signature _____

Address for Envelope

Drafting

• Write or type the first entry of your thank-you note and put it in your Writing Folder.

Objective: Students revise a thank-you note.

▶ **Writing a Thank-You Note**

Revising

Read the first draft of your thank-you note. Use the checklist to help you revise. Use editing and proofreading marks to make changes and corrections.

Proofreading Marks

Mark	Meaning
¶	Indent.
∧	Add something.
ℓ	Take out something.
≡	Make a capital letter.
/	Make a small letter.
sp	Check spelling.
⊙	Add a period.

Ideas

☐ Did you write the reason for the thank-you note?

☐ Are all the parts of a thank-you note included?

Organization

☐ Are the sentences in the order that best makes the note understood?

Word Choice

☐ Do you use prepositions to help show how, when, and where things happen?

☐ Do you add variety by using pronouns?

☐ Do all the verbs agree with the subjects?

Sentence Fluency

☐ Are all your sentences complete with subjects and predicates?

Voice

☐ Does your thank-you note sound friendly and polite?

If the revised draft of your thank-you note has many changes, write or type it and put it in your Writing Folder.

Objective: Students edit/proofread and publish a thank-you note.

UNIT 6 Country Life • **Lesson 6** *What Ever Happened to the Baxter Place?*

Writing a Thank-You Note

Editing/Proofreading

Edit/proofread your thank-you note on notebook paper or on a computer and put it in your Writing Folder. Read your thank-you note carefully. Use the checklist to help you correct any mistakes. Make your thank-you note easy to read and understand.

Conventions

☐ Did you use periods in titles?

☐ Did you use parentheses when adding extra information?

☐ Are all the names of people and places spelled correctly?

☐ Did you capitalize the greeting and the closing?

Publishing

Use the checklist to get your thank-you note ready to send.

Presentation

☐ Write or type a neat final copy of your thank-you note.

☐ Add a drawing, photograph, or computer graphic to add interest to your thank-you note.

☐ Address an envelope.

PERSONAL WRITING

UNIT 6 Country Life • **Lesson 7** *If you're not from the prairie...*

Writing Journal Entries

Objective: Students learn how to make journal entries.

Use the writing tips or the writing process to write journal entries.

Prewriting

Who is the audience for your journal entries?

☐ Yourself

☐ Your teacher

☐ Your classmates

☐ Your friends

☐ Your family

☐ Other _____

What is your purpose for writing these journal entries?

☐ To write out your ideas, thoughts, and feelings

☐ To explain your thoughts and feelings about something

☐ To share your ideas, thoughts, and feelings

☐ Other _____

What is the topic for your journal entry today?

_____

Name _____ Date _____

▶ **Writing Journal Entries**

Use the following graphic organizer or make one of your own to help you organize your journal entries.

Objective: Students learn how to make journal entries.

PERSONAL WRITING

⬭ **Journal Graphic Organizer** ⬭

_____ Date

_____

_____

_____ **Details**

_____

_____

_____

_____

_____

_____

. . . .

⬚ **Drafting** ⬚

• Write or type your journal entry and put it in your Writing Folder.

Objective: Students revise journal entries.

Writing Tips for Journal Entries

Writing Journal Entries

☐ Write entries in your journal every day.

☐ Set aside a special time for journal writing.

☐ Reread your journal often to get ideas.

☐ Drawings or photographs you add can also be sources for writing ideas.

Sharing Your Journal/Revising

Read your journal entries. Use the checklist to help you revise your writing. Use the editing and proofreading marks to make changes and corrections.

Proofreading Marks

∧	Add something.
ℓ	Take out something.
≡	Make a capital letter.
/	Make a small letter.
sp	Check spelling.
⊙	Add a period.

Ideas

☐ Are your ideas clearly stated?

Organization

☐ Can readers tell where one entry ends and the next one begins?

Word Choice

☐ Did you choose words that are specific?

Sentence Fluency

☐ Did you use a comma and a conjunction to make a compound sentence from two simple sentences?

Voice

☐ Do your journal entries sound like you are talking to a good friend?

If your revised journal has many changes, write or type it on notebook paper or on a computer and put it in your Writing Folder.

▶ **Writing Journal Entries**

PERSONAL WRITING

Objective: Students edit/proofread and publish journal entries.

More Writing Tips for Journal Entries

☐ Make sure you always have a pencil and paper.

☐ Many writers make journal entries in a notebook they can carry with them all the time.

☐ Journal entries do not always have to be writing ideas.

Sharing Your Journal/Editing and Publishing

Read your journal entries carefully. Use the checklist to help you correct any mistakes. Make your writing easy to read and understand.

Conventions

☐ Did you use colons correctly with lists and time?

☐ Did you use commas with interjections?

☐ Are all of the proper names capitalized?

Publishing

Use the checklist to get your journal ready to share.

Presentation

☐ Write or type a neat final copy of your journal entries.

☐ Add drawings or photographs to add interest to your journal.

☐ Practice reading your journal entries out loud if you plan to give an oral presentation.

Cumulative Checklists

Revising

Ideas

- [ ] Did I write a topic sentence for each paragraph?
- [ ] Do I stay on the topic?
- [ ] Did I include all of the details from my graphic organizer?
- [ ] Do I have an effective beginning?
- [ ] Is the main idea clear?
- [ ] Do my reasons, facts, and feelings support my main idea?
- [ ] Have I presented my idea in a new way?
- [ ] Did I capture my reader's interest?
- [ ] Did I give all the information I could?
- [ ] Does my writing have a beginning, middle, and end?
- [ ] Does the end sum up the story and keep the reader thinking?

Organization

- [ ] Did I include all of my ideas from prewriting?
- [ ] Does my beginning get the reader interested right away?
- [ ] Do I keep the same point of view throughout?
- [ ] Are lines, sentences, and paragraphs in the best order for reading and understanding?
- [ ] Does my topic sentence tell my reader what I want?
- [ ] Does my closing sentence sum up what I want? Does it give my most important reason?
- [ ] Did my facts or feelings support my main idea?
- [ ] Did I use the right pictures or drawings for my subject?
- [ ] Are my events in the correct time order?
- [ ] Does my ending wrap up the story?
- [ ] Did I remind my readers what I wanted them to do or think in the closing sentence?

Revising

Voice

☐ Does it sound like I know my subject well?

☐ Did I give facts, reasons, or feelings that I care about and that my reader will care about?

☐ Does my interest in my topic come across?

☐ Did I keep my audience in mind while I wrote?

Word Choice

☐ Are my words clear and specific?

☐ Did I use time and order words to help readers follow the order of events?

☐ Did I explain or define any uncommon words or terms?

☐ Do my place and location words make it clear to readers where people, things, and actions are?

☐ Are there any words that I have used too often?

☐ Did I use words my audience understands?

☐ Do my words create a picture for the reader?

☐ Have I used the correct tense of all my verbs? Do my verbs agree with the subjects? Did I use the correct main and helping verbs?

☐ Did I add variety by substituting pronouns for nouns?

Sentence Fluency

☐ Did I begin my sentences in different ways?

☐ Did I make some of my sentences long and some short?

☐ Do I have information that is repeated?

☐ Is there information that can be combined in one sentence?

☐ Are all my sentences complete with subjects and predicates?

☐ Did I use a comma and a conjunction to make a compound sentence out of two simple sentences?

Editing/Proofreading

Unit 1 Grammar

Lesson 1	☐	Nouns
Lesson 2	☐	Pronouns
Lesson 3	☐	Verbs—Action, State of Being, Linking
Lesson 4	☐	Verbs—Verb Phrase, Main Verb, Helping Verb
Lesson 5	☐	Sentences—Four Types
Lesson 6	☐	Review

Unit 2 Mechanics

Lesson 1	☐	Quotation Marks in Dialogue
Lesson 2	☐	Commas in a Series
Lesson 3	☐	Commas in Dialogue
Lesson 4	☐	Capitalization of Places—Cities, States, Countries, Parks, Buildings
Lesson 5	☐	Exclamation Points and Question Marks
Lesson 6	☐	Review

Unit 3 Usage

Lesson 1	☐	Sensory Adjectives
Lesson 2	☐	Contractions
Lesson 3	☐	Verb Tenses
Lesson 4	☐	Plural Nouns
Lesson 5	☐	Articles—Definite and Indefinite
Lesson 6	☐	Review

Unit 4 Grammar

Lesson 1	☐	Prepositions and Prepositional Phrases
Lesson 2	☐	Subjects and Predicates
Lesson 3	☐	Parenthesis; Periods in Abbreviations, Initials, Titles
Lesson 4	☐	Pronouns—Possessive, Singular and Plural

Editing/Proofreading

Lesson 5 ☐ Agreement—Singular and Plural, Regular and Irregular

Lesson 6 ☐ Adverbs—Comparative and Superlative

Lesson 7 ☐ Review

Unit 5 Mechanics

Lesson 1 ☐ Sentence Structure—Simple and Compound

Lesson 2 ☐ Colons—to Introduce Lists, between Hours and Minutes, in Business Letter Salutations

Lesson 3 ☐ Conjunctions and Interjections

Lesson 4 ☐ Capitalization—Greetings/Closings of Letters, Direct Quotes, Titles of Media, Titles of Written Works; Underlining—to set off the Titles of Books, Magazines, Newspapers, Television Shows, Movies, and Plays

Lesson 5 ☐ Capitalization—Proper Nouns, Titles, *I*, Initials of People, Words Used as Names, Acronyms, Names of Languages, Rivers, Oceans, Mountains

Lesson 6 ☐ Capitalization—Month and Year, Historic Periods, Special Events, Holidays

Lesson 7 ☐ Review

Unit 6 Grammar, Usage, and Mechanics

Lesson 1 ☐ Mechanics   Commas—in Dates, Friendly Letters, City/State/Country, after *yes/no*

Lesson 2 ☐ Mechanics   Apostrophes and Hyphens

Lesson 3 ☐ Grammar   Review of Unit 1

Lesson 4 ☐ Mechanics   Review of Unit 2

Lesson 5 ☐ Usage   Review of Unit 3

Lesson 6 ☐ Grammar   Review of Unit 4

Lesson 7 ☐ Mechanics   Review of Unit 5

Cumulative Checklists

Publishing

Unit 2 Expository Writing

☐ Write or type a neat final copy of your writing.

☐ Add a drawing, map, or use computer graphics to add interest to your writing.

☐ Practice reading your writing out loud if you plan to give an oral presentation.

Unit 3 Descriptive/Poetry

☐ Write or type a neat final copy of your writing.

☐ Add a drawing, map, or use computer graphics to add interest to your writing.

☐ Practice reading your writing out loud if you plan to give an oral presentation.

Unit 4 Persuasive Writing

☐ Make sure your writing says exactly what you want it to say.

☐ Make a clean copy of your writing. You may want to use the computer.

☐ Practice reading your writing out loud if you plan to give an oral presentation.

☐ Add drawings or pictures to make your writing more appealing.

Publishing

Unit 5 Narrative Writing

- ☐ Write or type a neat final copy of your writing.
- ☐ Make sure you have put in all the changes you made during revising and editing.
- ☐ Add photos or illustrations to your writing.
- ☐ Bind your writing in a book.
- ☐ Give your story a title.

Unit 6 Personal Writing

- ☐ Write or type a neat final copy of your writing.
- ☐ Add a drawing, photograph, or computer graphics to add interest.
- ☐ Practice reading your writing out loud if you plan to give an oral presentation.